FAMOUS NEW ORLEANS DRINKS
AND HOW TO MIX 'EM

CHRISTENING FONT OF THE COCKTAIL

The old-fashioned double-end egg-cup which served the first brandy-cocktails in old New Orleans. A *Coquetier* to the Creoles but a "cocktail" to the Americans.

FAMOUS NEW ORLEANS DRINKS
& how to mix'em

Stanley Clisby Arthur

Illustrated by GEORGE FORREST HOPKINS

PELICAN PUBLISHING COMPANY
GRETNA 2011

Printed in the United States of America
Published by Pelican Publishing Company, Inc.
1000 Burmaster Street, Gretna, Louisiana 70053

C O N T E N T S

Apéritif

Hail New Orleans that for more than a century has been the home of civilized drinking. From the time of its settlement by the French, through the domination of the Spanish, and occupation by the Americans after the Louisiana Purchase, the flowing bowl and the adept mixing of what went in it has constituted as high an art in this Creole city as the incomparable cooking for which it is famed.

The quality of mixed drinks as served in New Orleans has always appealed to the sophisticated taste, but the drinks and their histories are forever linked with the past of this pleasure-loving city out of which has come so much that is beautiful and gay, and so much that is worth preserving.

It was here that your pious Creole lady guilelessly brewed muscadine wine and blackberry cordial and peach brandy chocked with authority. It was here that your gentlemen of the old school, more or less pleasantly corned in season and out, made a cult of preparing a drink and a ritual of downing it. It was here that your most modern of American beverages, the cocktail, first came into being and was given its jaunty name.

With a desire to acquaint the world—or that part of the world that may be interested—with the art of mixing a drink as it is done in New Orleans, the author of this book has cajoled from old and new experts the recipes handed down through succeeding generations and presents them herein for your delectation with a smile and a *"Santé!"*

Why We Clink Glasses

(A Toast for Toasters)

When friends with other friends contrive
To make their glasses clink,
Then not one sense of all the five
Is absent from a drink.

For touch and taste and smell and sight
Evolve in pleasant round,
And when the flowing cups unite
We thrill to sense of sound.

Folly to look on wine? Oh, fie
On what teetotallers think . . .
There're always five good reasons why
Good fellows like to drink.

E. B. A.

The Birth of the Cocktail

The most popular alcoholic beverage in the world to-day is that high-powered mixture known as the Cocktail.

For a century and beyond this stimulating drink has served to elevate dejected spirits. Born, nurtured, and christened on this side of the Atlantic, it has overflowed its original boundaries, especially since the World War, and today even staid British taste, long wedded to historic brandy and soda, is beginning to find satisfaction —and something else—in the Yankee mixed drink.

Why is a cocktail called a cocktail? Why should the rear adornment of a chanticleer be identified with so robust a libation?

The origin of the cocktail and its singular naming have long been veiled in mystery. One legend sets forth that the French-speaking people of Old New Orleans had a word for a favorite drink, and that word eventually was corrupted into "cocktail." Other and more fanciful legends have found circulation from time to time but here are the facts concerning the birth of the cocktail and how it received its inapposite name.

In the year 1793, at the time of the uprising of the blacks on the portion of the island of San Domingo then belonging to France, wealthy white plantation owners were forced to flee that favored spot in the sun-lit Caribbean. With them went their precious belongings and heirlooms. Some of the expelled *Dominguois* who flocked to what was then Spanish Louisiana brought gold to New Orleans. Others brought slaves along with their household goods. Some brought nothing but the clothes they wore upon their backs. One refugee succeeded in salvaging, among other scanty possessions, a recipe for the compounding of a liquid tonic, called *bitters,* a recipe that had been a secret family formula for years.

This particular young Creole refugee was of a distinguished French family and had been educated as an apothecary. His name was Antoine Amedée Peychaud. In the turmoil of the insurrection and the hurried exodus from San Domingo, Amedée and his young sister, Lasthénie, became separated. It was not until years later when he had established himself in New Orleans, that the sister was located in Paris and Peychaud had her join him in his new home where subsequently she married into the well-known Maurin family.

A. A. Peychaud's bid for fame and popularity in the city of his adoption was founded not so much upon the quality or profusion of the drugs he dispensed over the counter of his shop (located in a building still standing at 437 Royal street) as upon his bitters, a tonic and stomachic compounded according to his secret family formula. These bitters, good for what ailed one irrespective of malady, gave an added zest to the potions of cognac brandy he served friends and others who came into his pharmacy—especially those in need of a little brandy, as well as bitters, for their stomach's sake.

The fame of Peychaud's highly flavored dram of brandy spread rapidly. Consequently the bitters found a ready market in the numerous coffee-houses (as liquid dispensing establishments were then called) that stood cheek by jowl in almost every street in old New Orleans. Cognac had long been a popular drink among the city's experienced bibbers, but presently customers began demanding their French brandy spiked with a dash or so of the marvelous bitters compounded by M. Peychaud.

In his own place of business Peychaud had a unique way of serving his spiced drink of brandy. He poured portions into what we now call an "egg-cup"—the old-fashioned double-end egg-cup. This particular piece of crockery, known to the French-speaking population as a *coquetier* (pronounced ko-k-tay'), was, in all probability, forerunner of the present jigger—the name given the double-end metal contraption holding a jigger (1½ ounces) in the big end, and a pony (1 ounce) in the little end, which we now use to measure portions for mixed drinks.

It is not surprising that those whose French pronunciation was imperfect were soon calling the spiced drink they quaffed from the big end of the crockery cup a "cock-tay." Possibly through sampling too many of M. Peychaud's spiced brandies, the thickened tongues of the imbibers slurred the word into "cocktail."

Presently all New Orleans was drinking brandy-cocktails, quite dissimilar indeed from the usual brandy-toddies heretofore served exclusively in most of the coffee-houses of old New Orleans. The bitters made the difference.

In such fashion did Peychaud's original San Domingo bitters give an otherwise simple brandy-toddy new life and zest. In such fashion did the inconspicuous little crockery *coquetier* or egg-cup become the christening font of the cocktail.

Many have been the yarns setting forth the correct etymology of the word "cocktail." Some of these legends are picturesque, some old, some modern, many fantastic, and most of them far-fetched and meaningless.

The word was not accepted by lexicographers until about the beginning of the present century, each pundit advancing a different version as to its origin. Dr. Frank H. Vizetelly, noted editor of the Standard Dictionary and authority on words, writes me;

"The *cocktail* goes back at least to the beginning of the 19th century, and may date back to the American Revolution. It is alleged by one writer to have been a concoction prepared by the widow of a Revolutionary soldier as far back as 1779. He offers no proof of the statement, but a publication, *The Balance,* for May 13, 1806, describes the *cocktail* of that period as 'a stimulating liquor composed of spirits of any kind, sugar, water, and bitters. It is vulgarly called *bitter sling,* and is supposed to be an excellent electioneering potion.'

"Washington Irving in *Knickerbocker* (1809), page 241, said of the *cocktail*: 'They (Dutch-Americans) lay claim to be the first inventors of the recondite beverages, *cock-tail, stone-fence,* and *sherry-cobbler.*' Hawthorne referred to *cocktails* in *The Blithedale Romance* (1852), as did Thackeray in his *The Newcomes* (1854), but neither of these authors shed any light upon the origin of the term.

"*The New England Dictionary on Historical Principles* says that the origin of the word *cocktail* is lost. In this connection one writer refers to the older term *cocktail,* meaning a horse whose tail, being docked, sticks up like the tail of a cock. He adds: 'Since drinkers of cocktails believe them to be exhilarating, the recently popular song "Horsy, keep your tail up," may perhaps hint at a possible connection between the two senses of "cocktail".'

"Bartlett in his *Dictionary of Americanisms* gives the following: '*Cocktail*. A stimulating beverage, made of brandy, gin, or other liquor, mixed with bitters, sugar and a very little water. A friend thinks this term was suggested by the shape which the froth, as a glass of porter, assumes when it flows over the sides of a tumbler containing the liquid effervescing.' He quotes the following from the *New York Tribune* of May 8, 1862: 'A bowie-knife and a foaming cocktail.' In Yorkshire dialect, *cocktail* describes beer that is fresh and foaming.

"Brewer in *A Dictionary of Phrase and Fable*, following the definition of *cocktail*, adds the note: 'The origin of the term is unknown: the story given in the New York World (1891) to the effect that it is an Aztec word, and that "the liquor was discovered by a Toltec noble, who sent it by the hand of his daughter Xochitl," to the king who promptly named it "xoctl," whence "cocktail" is a good specimen of the manufacture of popular etymologies.'

"As you will see from the foregoing, altho many theories have been advanced as to the etymology of the term *cocktail*, these, like most etymologies of the kind, are mere flights of fancy, and while they make interesting reading, cannot be accepted as reliable."

After careful analysis of Doctor Vizetelly's data it appears to be certain that the odd mispronunciation of *coquetier* in New Orleans is the oldest and most positive basis for the word "cocktail."

Monsieur Peychaud, glass in hand we salute you! *A votre santé!*

An interesting tale bearing upon the use of the word cocktail in Old New Orleans is to be found in a book written by a German traveler over a century ago. The author was Henry Didimus, and his book, *New Orleans As I Saw It*, tells of his adventures in the Crescent City in the winter of 1835-36 at which time he became acquainted with the then famed brandy-cocktail.

Herr Didimus writes of wandering about the old town and of meeting up with three worthies . . . "one played the fiddle, another beat the drum, and the third dealt out nectar in the form of brandy-cocktail." Didimus says he repeated the name, "brandy-cocktail" when such a drink was suggested, so as to gain the attention of the third worthy who thereupon said: "Ah, I see; not acquainted with the mixture," and led the way to a refreshment place. When all were seated about a table, the third worthy yelled: "Boy, bring up four glasses of brandy-cocktails!"

The black slave vanished and returned with four tumblers practically filled, each of Didimus' companions seized a glass, and eyes shining with anticipation, glasses were touched, and the drinks were downed.

Herr Didimus, immensely pleased with what the draft did to his insides, demanded to be told in what way a brandy-*cocktail* differed from a brandy-*toddy?*

"The difference between a brandy-cocktail and a brandy-toddy is this," explained the loquacious worthy. "A brandy-toddy is made by adding together a little water, a little sugar, and a great deal of brandy—mix well and drink. A brandy-cocktail is composed of the same ingredients, with the addition of a shade of bitters —so that the bitters draw the line of demarkation. Boy!" he bellowed, "bring up four brandy-toddies—you shall taste the difference, sir!"

Whiskey Drinks

Whiskey is a potent drink and whiskey is a potent word—perhaps because both are of Irish extraction. The English pronunciation of the word in use today is based upon a word the ancient Gaels applied to the product of their stills, for it appears they were the original whiskey-makers.

The name they gave the distilled spirit was singularly fitting—they called it *uisgebeatha.* If we dissect the word we find that *uisge* (pronounced *oosh'gee*) means "water," *beatha* means "life," and the two combined mean "water of life." All of which goes to prove you can't beat the Irish for apt naming. In time this potent product of Ould Ireland's stills became "whiskbae," later "whiskie," and finally just plain "whiskey."

The Scots likewise were distillers of this ancient and honorable liquid. They adopted the original name the Irish gave to the white spirit which flowed from their stills, the word going through a similar sequence of pronunciation until it became "whisky" without the e — note spelling on any bottle of Scotch.

We have much for which to thank the Irish, but whiskey rates a top place on the list. A toast to the Irish! And what drink may better serve such purpose than one of the many whiskey cocktails mixed to perfection as in New Orleans? Make it an Old Fashioned, a Sazerac, a Manhattan, a julep, a highball, or just plain whiskey. Whichever it may be, fill 'em up and drink 'em down to the original whiskey-makers—the Irish!

Highballs

```
1 jigger rye whiskey,
           or,
           Bourbon whiskey,
           Scotch whisky,
           Irish whiskey,
           cognac brandy,
           applejack,
           gin,
           rum.
      fizz water
      ice
```

The dictionary lowdown on highball: "a long drink of diluted spirits, usually whiskey, served in a tall glass with cracked ice."

Like all popular drinks, the highball is conspicuous for its variety. Any spirituous liquor will answer—it depends upon individual preference. Some like rye with seltzer water, some Bourbon; others hold that the spirit of the drink should be Scots whisky, and still others demand Irish whiskey. Brandy, rum, applejack, all have their advocates, and there are even benighted souls who crave gin in their highballs.

As they used to say out West: "Name your own poison, gents!"

For the fizz accompaniment use whichever of these appeals to you—seltzer, club soda, white rock, ginger ale, coca cola, seven-up. Connoisseurs, as a rule, insist that only cold water be poured upon their whiskey.

The Sazerac Cocktail

Oldtimers will tell you the three outstanding drinks of New Orleans in the memory of living men were the dripped absinthe frappé of the Old Absinthe House, the Ramos gin fizz, and the Sazerac cocktail.

As previously related, the American cocktail was not only born in Old New Orleans but was given its curious name in the city's famous *Vieux Carré*. There are cocktails and cocktails but the best known of all New Orleans cocktails is unquestionably the Sazerac. The fact that it originated in New Orleans gave rise to the legend that it was first concocted by and named for an old Louisiana family, legend without fact as no such Louisiana family ever existed.

A barbershop now holds forth in a building on the right hand side of the first block in Royal street going down from Canal, and before its doors, still remains lettered in the sidewalk the word "SAZERAC." This denotative indicated the entranceway to a once well-patronized bar on the Exchange Alley side of the building. It was here the drink famed far and wide as a Sazerac cocktail was mixed and dispensed. It was here it was christened with the name it now bears.

For years one of the favorite brands of cognac imported

into New Orleans was a brand manufactured by the firm of *Sazerac-de-Forge et fils,* of Limoges, France. The local agent for this firm was John B. Schiller. In 1859 Schiller opened a liquid dispensary at 13 Exchange Alley, naming it "Sazerac Coffee-house" after the brand of cognac served exclusively at his bar.

Schiller's brandy cocktails became the drink of the day and his business flourished, surviving even the War Between the States. In 1870 Thomas H. Handy, his bookkeeper, succeeded as proprietor and changed the name to "Sazerac House." An alteration in the mixture also took place. Peychaud's bitters was still used to add the right fillip, but American rye whiskey was substituted for the cognac to please the tastes of Americans who preferred "red likker" to any pale-faced brandy.

Thus brandy vanished from the Sazerac cocktail to be replaced by whiskey (Handy always used Maryland Club rye, if you are interested in brand names), and the dash of absinthe was added. Precisely when whiskey replaced brandy and the dash of absinthe added are moot questions. The absinthe innovation has been credited to Leon Lamothe who in 1858 was a bartender for Emile Seignouret, Charles Cavaroc & Co., a wine importing firm located in the old Seignouret mansion still standing at 520 Royal street. More likely it was about 1870, when Lamothe was employed at Pina's restaurant in Burgundy street that he experimented with absinthe and made the Sazerac what it is today.

But this history delving is dry stuff, so let's sample a genuine Sazerac. We will ask Leon Dupont, now vice-president of the St. Regis Restaurant but for years one of the expert cocktail mixers behind Tom Handy's original Sazerac bar, to make one for us.

Here's how—and how!

1 lump sugar
3 drops Peychaud's bitters
1 dash Angostura bitters
1 jigger *rye* whiskey
1 dash absinthe substitute
1 slice lemon peel

To mix a Sazerac requires two heavy-bottomed, 3½-ounce bar glasses. One is filled with cracked ice and allowed to chill. In the other a lump of sugar is placed with just enough water to moisten it. The saturated loaf of sugar is then crushed with a barspoon. Add a few drops of Peychaud's bitters, a dash of Angostura, a jigger of *rye* whiskey, for while Bourbon may do for a julep it just won't do for a real Sazerac. To the glass containing sugar, bitters, and rye add several lumps of ice and stir. Never use a shaker! Empty the first glass of its ice, dash in several drops of absinthe, twirl the glass and shake out the absinthe . . . enough will cling to the glass to give the needed flavor. Strain into this glass the whiskey mixture, twist a piece of lemon peel over it for the needed zest of that small drop of oil thus extracted from the peel, but do not commit the sacrilege of dropping the peel into the drink. Some bartenders put a cherry in a Sazerac; very pretty but not necessary.

M-m-m-m-m! Let's have another, Leon!

Kentucky Whiskey Cocktail

1 jigger Bourbon whiskey
1 jigger unsweetened pineapple juice
1 lump sugar

Dissolve the sugar in the pineapple juice. Pour in the jigger of Bourbon. Then some lumps of ice. Stir. Strain in serving glass.

This cocktail could be made with rye whiskey, but then you'd not be privileged to attach the name Kentucky to it. Some make the same drink with orange juice instead of pineapple, and some use sweetened pineapple juice. If the latter, be wary of the amount of sugar you use.

Old Fashioned Cocktail

1 lump sugar
2 dashes Peychaud or Angostura bitters
1 jigger *rye* whiskey
1 piece lemon peel
1 chunk pineapple
1 slice orange peel
2 maraschino cherries

Into a heavy-bottomed barglass drop a lump of sugar, dash on the bitters, and crush with a spoon. Pour in the jigger of rye whiskey and stir with several lumps of ice. No shaking allowed! Let the mixture remain in the glass in which it is prepared. Garnish with a half-ring of orange peel, add the chunk of pineapple, and the cherries with a little of the maraschino juice. Twist the slice of lemon peel over all and serve in the mixing glass with the barspoon.

Old Fashioned? Yea, verily, but as appealing to smart tastes now as on that certain Derby Day a half century ago when the originator, whoever he may have been, first stirred it into being at the Pendennis Club, in Louisville, Kentucky.

The Old Fashioned has been a New Orleans institution for many years and when other whiskey mixtures, garnished with fancy names, have passed on and been forgotten, the Old Fashioned will continue to tickle experienced palates. Don't let anyone tell you that gin, rum, or brandy can take the place of whiskey in an Old Fashioned. Turn a deaf ear to such heresy. A real Old Fashioned demands rye whiskey. Remember, Bourbon won't do.

In the old days before the Great Mistake the Old Fashioned contained less fruit than it does today. Howbeit, the expert barkeep of pre-prohibition days never neglected to twist a slice of lemon peel over the glass before serving.

Blue Blazer

1 lump sugar
1 jigger Scotch whisky
1 jigger hot water

Have two mugs, earthenware or metal, and in one dissolve the lump of sugar in the hot water. Now add the Scots whisky; be sure it's a good brand with plenty of alcoholic content for it has to burn. Ignite the mixture. Hold the burning mug in one hand, then empty the fluid rapidly from one container to the other so that a streak of blue flame connects the two. Serve in a hot-drink glass after twisting a bit of lemon peel over the mixture and topping with a grating of nutmeg.

If you have cold feet, chattering teeth, shivers, frozen fingers, or chilblains, in other words, if you're cold, and want to warm up the inner man, you can do no better than thaw out with a Blue Blazer.

This drink was a popular tipple aboard the palatial paddle-wheeled steamboats that churned the waters of the Mississippi during the time the *Natchez* and the *Robert E. Lee* made history in upstream races to Saint Louis. The barkeeps were expert in transferring the blue-flamed liquid from one mug to another, accomplishing the feat with an agility that kept the flames from singeing their walrus-like moustaches. You can do the same, (with or without the moustaches) but be cautious; if any of this hot Scotch gets on your fingers they'll burn like blue blazes!

Manhattan Cocktail

1 lump sugar
1 dash Peychaud bitters
1 dash Angostura bitters
½ jigger rye whiskey
½ jigger Italian vermouth
1 slice lemon peel

Drop a lump of sugar in a barglass, moisten with a very little water, dash on it the two bitters, and crush with a barspoon. Add the rye whiskey (don't use Bourbon) and then the vermouth. Drop several lumps of ice into the glass and *stir*. After straining into the cocktail glass, twist a bit of lemon peel over the mixture to extract the atom of oil, drop in a maraschino cherry with a very little of the sirup.

There are almost as many recipes for a real Manhattan cocktail as there are skyscrapers in Little Old New York, or ways of getting into heaven. The Manhattan, originated at the old Delmonico Restaurant in New York during the bibulous 90's, was composed of one-third Italian vermouth, and two-thirds Bourbon whiskey. Naturally, the formula has been improved upon in New Orleans; you'll note we always improve upon things to eat and drink in this New Orleans. Just an old Southern custom!

The Manhattan as served over the better New Orleans bars has always had that certain something it lacks elsewhere. Reason: in first-class establishments the mixologists use rye for the whiskey and the drink is stirred— never shaken. Properly mixed with good brands of liquor, the Manhattan is one of the finest drinks that flourishes under the name of cocktail, and well deserves the reputation that "it is the most popular cocktail in the world."

Dry Manhattan

1 lump sugar
1 dash Peychaud bitters
1 dash Angostura bitters
1/3 jigger rye whiskey
1/3 jigger Italian vermouth
1/3 jigger French vermouth
1 slice lemon peel

This is mixed exactly as is the Manhattan. Must not be shaken —a brisk stirring with large lumps of ice is the proper procedure. Fine or crushed ice has a tendency to make drinks cloudy and whiskey cocktails should have a clear amber color. Put a cherry in the cocktail glass before straining in the mixture.

There are cocktail quaffers who object to the sweetness of the Manhattan made in the orthodox manner and prefer a *dry* Manhattan. The dryer drink is made by using a third of a jigger each of the rye, the Italian, and the French vermouths. When dropping the cherry into the cocktail glass do not include any of the sirup.

Whiskey Cocktail

1 lump sugar
6-7 drops Angostura bitters
5-6 drops Peychaud bitters
1 teaspoon curaçao
1 jigger rye whiskey

Use a heavy-bottomed barglass and drop in a lump of sugar. Moisten with a little water, add the two bitters, then crush with a spoon. Put in the curaçao, then the jigger of rye, and stir with several lumps of ice. Strain into the serving glass. Finally twist a sliver of lemon peel over the mixture. That adds the tiny drop of oil necessary for the perfect result.

The whiskey cocktail is one of the old-time appetizer drinks masquerading under a variety of names in different parts of the country. Follow this recipe and you will agree it's a cocktail deserving its wide popularity.

Cocktail à la Louisiane

1/3 jigger rye whiskey
1/3 jigger Italian vermouth
1/3 jigger Benedictine
3-4 dashes absinthe substitute
3-4 dashes Peychaud bitters

Mix in barglass with lumps of ice. Strain into a cocktail glass in which has been placed a maraschino cherry.

This is the special cocktail served at *Restaurant de la Louisiane*, one of the famous French restaurants of New Orleans, long the rendezvous of those who appreciate the best in Creole cuisine. *La Louisiane* cocktail is as out-of-the-ordinary as the many distinctive dishes that grace its menu.

Orange Whiskey Cocktail

1 jigger rye whiskey
1 jigger orange juice
1 jigger charged water
1 dash Peychaud bitters
1 lump sugar

Mix the ingredients in a barglass, pour into a shaker with crushed ice and shake vigorously. Strain into chilled cocktail glass. Prepare in generous quantities, for your guests will offer their glasses for more.

While rye is indicated in the recipe you may substitute Bourbon if that is your choice . . . but sidestep Scotch or Irish. The addition of the carbonated water gives this one a little more sparkle than if you use plain water.

The same cocktail can be made by substituting Orange Wine for the orange juice. In some New Orleans homes the celebrated Louisiana Orange Wine, made in the orange groves below the city, is used in preference to the plain orange juice. Many experts prefer Bourbon to rye in this particular cocktail.

Place d'Armes Cocktail

½ orange—juice only
½ lemon—juice only
½ lime—juice only
1 pony grenadine sirup
1 jigger whiskey

Squeeze the fruit juices in a mixing glass. Add the sirup; be careful not to make it too sweet if you like a dry drink . . . Otherwise use a little sugar. Then add the whiskey—some prefer Bourbon, others rye. Rye is usually better in any mixed drink. Strain into a tall glass half-filled with crushed ice. Decorate with a sprig of mint, after frappéing well with a spoon.

Of course, this gallant cocktail might be called a Jackson Square as readily as a *Place d'Armes* or, if you speak Spanish, how about *Plaza de Armas?* But its originator called it a *Place d'Armes,* and we'll stick to that. It was so named in honor of the grassy tree-shaded square fronting the Cathedral and the Cabildo, where General Andrew Jackson sits astride a rearing battle steed, holding aloft his chapeau in perpetual politeness. He would have enjoyed this cocktail!

Roffignac Cocktail

1 jigger whiskey
1 pony sirup
seltzer or soda water
raspberry sirup

Pour into a highball glass the jigger of whiskey (or use cognac, as in the original drink). Add the sirup, which may be raspberry, grenadine, or red Hembarig, the sweetening used in New Orleans a century ago. Add the soda water. Ice, of course.

Joseph Roffignac, before he fled his native land of France at the time of the Revolution, was Count Louis Philippe Joseph de Roffignac. In time he became a leading merchant in New Orleans, the city of his adoption, and its mayor for eight years. He fought the British under "Old Hickory" at the Battle of New Orleans, served in the state legislature, and was a banker of note. As mayor he introduced street lighting, and laid the first cobblestones in Royal street. For all his many honors, Roffignac's name comes to us through the years linked with a favorite tipple of Old New Orleans—the Roffignac.

While not so celebrated as A. A. Peychaud's cocktail, it was equally potent. The red Hembarig mentioned in the directions for mixing was a popular sirup when old New Orleans was young.

Juleps

The word julep is an old and honored one and can be traced as far back as A. D. 1400—long before we ever heard of the Southern States of these United States, where the julep is popularly supposed to be indigenous.

For centuries the julep has been described as "something to cool or assuage the heat of passion," and "a sweet drink prepared in different ways." We know nothing of the first definition but will confirm the second statement that it can be made in different ways.

The earliest form of the word was *iulep*. Arabs called it *julab*, the Portuguese *julepe*, the Italians *giulebbe*, Latins named it *julapium*, Persians, *gul-ab*, meaning "rose water." The Greeks, alas, did *not* have a word for it! *Julep*, as we spell it, is French. All this being settled, let us get on with our juleping.

Don't use rye whiskey in making a julep. If you do use whiskey let it be Bourbon, which serves its highest purpose when it becomes a component part of that prince of all thirst-quenchers known as the Mint Julep. There are many kinds of mint juleps, one for nearly every Southern State—such as Kentucky, Georgia, Virginia, Maryland, Louisiana juleps. We give several of the most popular recipes.

*"The first thing he did upon getting out of bed was to call for
a Julep and I date my own love for whiskey from mixing and
tasting my young master's juleps." 1804.*

Mint Julep

1 teaspoon sugar
1 dozen mint leaves
1 jigger Bourbon whiskey
1 pony rum

Put the mint leaves into a tall glass in which the julep is to be served. Add the sugar and crush in a little water. Pour in the Bourbon whiskey, then the rum, and fill the glass with shaved ice. Jiggle the mixture with a long-handled spoon (do not stir) until the outside of the glass or metal goblet is heavily frosted. Arrange a bouquet of several sprigs of mint on top just before handing to the recipient, who will ever after bless you.

Naturally, one is aware that he takes his life in his hands by even suggesting the way a *real* mint julep should be prepared, for there are as many recipes for this truly Southern drink as there are southern states in the Union.

Julep experts—may their tribe never decrease!—know that correct and authentic recipes take on changes in passing from one state to another. Southern colonels, to say nothing of majors, captains, and buck privates, have been known to call for pistols under the duelling oaks when it is even hinted that mint leaves be crushed in preparing a julep. Other colonels, majors, etc., emit fire and brimstone, and a Bourbon-laden breath, if the pungent leaves are not crushed in the bottom of the glass and a bouquet of short-to-measure sprigs placed on top in which to snuggle the nose while the nectar is being withdrawn with a reverent, albeit, audible sucking through a straw.

There is also a difference of opinion concerning the variety of spirits that go into the making. In the recipe above the pony of rum may be added or subtracted—it all depends on your drinking mathematics. Rum, however, gives added zest to a regulation whiskey julep.

Twenty-eight

The one thing upon which the two mint julep schools are fully agreed is this: it was a julep the two Carolina governors had in mind when making their celebrated observation regarding the length of time between drinks.

Kentucky Mint Julep

1 lump loaf sugar
? sprigs of mint leaves
? jiggers Bourbon whiskey

Note the absence of the amount of Bourbon to be used—that's important in a julep, no matter from what state it comes. All that is lacking in the above recipe is the shaved ice which must go into the glass or metal goblet in which the julep is compounded.

While Georgia may be able to make good the boast that the mint julep originated within her borders, there appears to be no successful refutation of Kentucky's claim that the Blue Grass State popularized the famous drink. However divided opinion as to whether mint leaves should be crushed or merely dunked, one thing is certain—no Kentucky gentleman, far less a Kentucky colonel, would ever sanction a recipe which placed limitations on the amount of Bourbon that goes into the making.

Nor will we here entangle ourselves in the age-long controversy—should a julep be sucked through a straw or drunk from the container? Kentuckians vociferously maintain that the use of a straw ruins a julep. We have tried Kentucky julep with a straw and without—both work!

On one of his many visits to New Orleans "Marse Henry" Watterson, one-time beloved editor of the Louisville *Courier-Journal,* told a young newspaper reporter his recipe for a real Kentucky mint julep.

"Take a silver goblet, son, one that will hold at least a pint, and dissolve a lump of loaf sugar in it with not more than a tablespoon of water. Take one mint leaf, no more, and crush it gently between the thumb and forefinger before dropping it into the dissolved sugar. Then fill the goblet nearly to the brim with shaved ice. Pour into it all the Bourbon whiskey the goblet will hold. Take a few sprigs of mint leaves and use for decorating the top of the mixture, after it has been well frappéd with a spoon. Then drink it. But," warned Marse Henry, "do not use a straw, son."

I know that this was Marse Henry's version of a real Kentucky mint julep, for I was the young—and thirsty —newspaper reporter.

Georgia Mint Julep

    1 teaspoon powdered sugar
    1 pony cognac brandy
    1 pony peach brandy
      sprigs of tender mint shoots

Use the goblet in which the julep is to be served. Place some of the mint leaves at the bottom, with the sugar and a little water, and muddle or bruise the leaves. Add the cognac and peach brandy. Fill the goblet with finely crushed ice. Jiggle with the long-handled barspoon until well frappéd.

Jiggling is not "stirring." Stirring calls for a rotary motion, but "jiggling" is dashing the spoon up and down steadily until the outside of the goblet is frosted. Place the metal or glass container on a table to do your jiggling —do not hold the glass for heat of the hand will hinder frost from forming on the outside. When the julep has been thoroughly jiggled, thrust in a bunch of the tenderest mint shoots arranged to simulate a bouquet.

This julep is to be absorbed with a straw, a short one so that the drinker's nose is buried in the very heart of the green nosegay as he drinks, thus adding the delight of aroma to the delight of taste.

San Domingo Julep

1 piece of loaf sugar
1½ jigger rum
sprigs of mint

Into a tall glass (preferably a metal goblet) drop the sugar and moisten with a little water. Take several mint leaves and crush while the sugar is being muddled with the barspoon. Fill with shaved or finely crushed ice. Pour in the rum. Jiggle to frappé the mixture. Set a bouquet of mint leaves on top before serving. A slice of orange peel for garnish is ritzy but not strictly necessary.

This seems to be the original mint julep that came to Louisiana away back in 1793, at the time the white aristocrats, who were expelled from San Domingo by the uprising of the blacks, settled in New Orleans. In the United States, especially those states south of the Mason and Dixon line, Bourbon whiskey gradually took the place of sugar cane rum as the spirit of the drink.

Many advocate the use of both red whiskey and rum in making a julep, but if you wish to quaff the original San Domingo julep use rum alone. Any of the well-known imported or domestic brands will do, such as Bacardi, Cabildo, Carioca, Pontalba, Rumrico, Charleston, Don Q., Puerto Rico, Jamaica, St. Croix, Red Heart, or Pilgrim.

Thirty-one

Brandy Mint Julep

1 spoon powdered sugar
1 pony Bourbon whiskey
1 pony peach brandy
sprigs of mint leaves

Mix as directed for the juleps in preceding pages. Use plenty of crushed ice and frappé with the long-handled barspoon.

It is rank heresy even to mention it, but some Georgia julep experts make theirs by substituting Bourbon whiskey for cognac brandy. Whichever you use, Bourbon or brandy, remember that quicker and prettier frosting will result if you use a silver or other metal goblet rather than glass. The outside of the container must be kept dry if it is to take on a good frost, so do not hold it in your hand when jiggling.

St. Regis Mint Julep

1 teaspoon sugar
1 teaspoon water
1 dozen mint leaves
1 jigger *rye* whiskey
½ pony rum
1 dash grenadine sirup

Into a tall glass crush the mint leaves with a barspoon. Dissolve the sugar in water and stir. Pour in the whiskey and rum, then the grenadine sirup. Fill the glass with crushed ice and jiggle with the spoon. When properly frappéd decorate the top with sprigs of mint.

This recipe departs in two ways from the usual . . . the use of rye for Bourbon and the introduction of grenadine sirup. In spite of its straying from the neither straight nor narrow path of Bourbon, this julep is exceedingly good on a hot day, or any day, for that matter. It is the julep that is served at the St. Regis Restaurant bar and is the pride of head-bartender John Swago.

Louisiana Mint Julep

1 teaspoon powdered sugar
1½ jigger Bourbon whiskey
sprigs of mint
crushed ice

Put a dozen leaves of mint in a barglass, cover with powdered sugar and just enough water to dissolve the sugar. Crush sugar and mint leaves gently with a muddler or barspoon. Pour half the mint and sugar liquid in the bottom of the tall glass in which the julep is to be served. Then enough shaved or snowball ice to half fill. Next add the remaining mint and sugar liquid, fill nearly to the top with shaved ice. Pour in the Bourbon until the glass is full to the brim. Place in the refrigerator at least an hour before serving to acquire ripeness and frost. Top with mint sprigs.

Time was when the mint julep was strictly a symbol of the South—a green and silver emblem of Dixie's friendly leisure. But today the mint julep, that most glorious of summer drinks, is becoming as popular above the Mason and Dixon line as below it.

Some term the Louisiana julep the last word in perfection, so if you have the feeling you haven't sampled a real julep, try the above. If you are still in doubt and are willing to go to some trouble, try the one below.

New Orleans Mint Julep

Put the glasses or the metal goblets in the refrigerator the night before you are to serve juleps. This is a high-powered julep so you'll need two jiggers of Bourbon for every glass. In the serving glass drop a layer of mint leaves, fill one-quarter full with shaved or snowball ice, then one teaspoon of powdered sugar. Repeat until the glass is half full. Add one jigger of Bourbon. Repeat until the glass is full, the second jigger of Bourbon being the last to go into the glass. Serve on a tray with a straw or tube in each goblet so that hand does not touch the container, which is frosted white.

Thirty-three

"Thy secret pleasure turns to open shame, thy sugred tongue to bitter wormwood tast." Shakespeare's Lucrece. 1593.

Absinthe Drinks

According to some authorities, absinthe as a drink originated in Algeria, and French soldiers serving in the Franco-Algerian war (1830-47) introduced the green spirits to Paris upon their return from the North African country where the drink found strong favor along the boulevards. In time the spectacle of bearded men and demi-mondes *dripping* their absinthes became one of the sights of Paris. Naturally, so fashionable a Parisian drink was not long in finding its way to the Little Paris of North America—New Orleans.

The drink, which was spelled *absynthe* in New Orleans liquor advertisements in 1837, when it was apparently first imported from France and Switzerland, was a liquor distilled from a large number of various herbs, roots, seeds, leaves, and barks steeped in anise. It also included *Artemisia asbinthium,* a herb known as "Wormwood" abroad, but called *Herbe Sainte* by the French-speaking population of Louisiana. In recent years wormwood has been condemned as harmful and habit-forming, and laws have been enacted forbidding its use in liquors in the United States and other countries. In addition to banning wormwood from manufactured liquor, the use of the word "absinthe" on bottles of modern concoctions which do not contain wormwood, is also banned. As a consequence, manufacturers of absinthe substitutes have been forced to adopt trade names.

Old Absinthe House

Of all the ancient buildings in New Orleans' famed *Vieux Carré,* none has been more glorified in story and picture than a square, plastered-brick building at the corner of Bourbon and Bienville streets, known as "The Old Absinthe House."

Hoary legend has long set forth that the building was erected in 1752, 1774, 1786, 1792, but as a matter of fact it was actually built in 1806 for the importing and commission firm of Juncadella & Font, Catalonians from Barcelona, Spain. In 1820, after Francisco Juncadella died and Pedro Font returned to his native land, the place continued as a commission house for the barter of foodstuffs, tobacco, shoes, clothing, as well as liquids in bulk from Spain, and was conducted by relatives of the builders. Later it became an *epicerie,* or grocery shop; for several years it was a *cordonnerie,* or boot and shoe store, and not until 1846 did the ground floor corner room become a coffee-house, as saloons were then called.

This initial liquid-refreshment establishment was run by Jacinto Aleix, a nephew of Señora Juncadella, and was known as "Aleix's Coffee-House." In 1869, Cayetano Ferrér, a Catalan from Barcelona, who had been a bar-keeper at the French Opera House, transferred his talents to the old Juncadella *casa* and became principal drink-mixer for the Aleix brothers. In 1874, Cayetano himself leased the place, calling it the "Absinthe Room" because of the potent dripped absinthe he served in the Parisian manner. His drink became so popular that it won fame not only for Cayetano, but for the balance of his family as well—papa, mamma, Uncle Leon, and three sons, Felix, Paul, and Jacinto, who helped to attend the wants of all and sundry who crowded the place. What the customers came for chiefly was the emerald liquor into which, tiny drop by tiny drop, fell water from the brass faucets of the pair of fountains that decorated the long cypress bar. These old fountains, relics of a romantic past, remained in the *Casa Juncadella* for many years. Came prohibition when the doors of "The Old Absinthe House" were padlocked by a United States marshal, and the contents of the place went under the hammer. Pierre Cazebonne purchased the prized antiques, together with the old bar, and set them up in another liquid refreshment parlor a block farther down Bourbon street, where signs now inform the tourist that therein is to be found the original "Old Absinthe Bar" and antique fountains, and we find the marble bases pitted from the water which fell, drop by drop, from the faucets over the many years they served their glorious mission.

In these modern years the tourist yearning for an old flavor of the Old New Orleans to carry back as a memory of his visit, goes to 400 Bourbon street, not only to see the venerable fountains and bar, but to be served absinthe frappé by a son of Cayetano Ferrér, the Spaniard who established "The Old Absinthe House." Jacinto Ferrér (we who know him call him "Josh") should indeed know how to prepare the drink properly for he has been at it 65 years. Josh served his apprenticeship in his father's celebrated "Absinthe Room" in 1872, and today at three-score-years-and-ten, carries on with an air the profession at which he began his apprenticeship as a five-year-old boy.

Dripped Absinthe Française

1 lump sugar
1 jigger absinthe substitute
1 glass cracked ice

Pour the jigger of absinthe substitute into a barglass filled with cracked ice. Over it suspend a lump of sugar in a special absinthe glass which has a small hole in the bottom (use a strainer if you haven't the glass) and allow water to drip, drop by drop, slowly into the sugar. When the desired color which indicates its strength has been reached and most of the sugar dissolved, stir with a spoon to frappé. Strain into a serving glass.

This recipe is for the original dripped absinthe that made famous Cayetano Ferrér's "Old Absinthe House" when he introduced the Parisian drink to New Orleans —the drink containing oil of wormwood which instigated the banishing of the word "Absinthe" from bottle labels. It is the same dripped absinthe, the "Fairy with Green Eyes," described in Marie Corelli's famous book "Wormwood."

Today, the absinthe substitutes are free of the harmful extract of the herb *Artemisia absinthium,* and entirely safe when imbibed (in moderation) at any bar.

Absinthe Cocktail

1 jigger absinthe substitute
1 teaspoon sugar sirup
1 dash anisette
2 dashes Peychaud bitters
2 ounces charged water

Fill a highball glass a little more than half full with cracked or crushed ice. Pour in the absinthe substitute, sugar sirup, anisette, and bitters, then squirt in carbonated or other live water. Jiggle with a barspoon until the mixture is well frappéd. Strain into cocktail glasses which have been iced ahead of time.

Absinthe Frappé

1 jigger absinthe substitute
1 teaspoon sugar sirup
1 jigger charged water.

Fill a small highball glass with cracked or shaved ice. Pour in the sugar sirup, then the absinthe substitute, and drip water (seltzer or other charged water will improve it) slowly while frappéing with the spoon. Continue jiggling the barspoon until the glass becomes well frosted.

This is the simple and easy way to prepare an absinthe drink, one that has many devotees in many lands. Of course, if you have a shiny cocktail shaker and want to put it to work, you can use it. Shake until the shaker takes on a good coating of frost, and then pour the mixture into glasses which have been well iced before the drink is prepared.

Absinthe Anisette

1 pony anisette
1 jigger absinthe substitute

Use a small glass and fill with shaved or finely cracked ice. Pour in the anisette and absinthe. Jiggle with a barspoon until heavily frappéd and serve in the same glass. A straw goes with this one.

The modern absinthe substitutes cannot be detected in taste even by those who were familiar with the original but now illegal liquor, a flood of fancy and trademarked names has resulted, and it is marketed under such names as Greenopal, Herbsaint, Pernod, Assent, Milky Way, and the like.

Green Opal Cocktail

> 1 jigger Greenopal, or other absinthe
> substitute
> ½ pony dry gin
> ½ pony anisette or ojen
> 1 dash orange bitters
> 2 dashes Peychaud bitters

Put the absinthe substitute and dry gin in a shaker. Add anisette or ojen (make your own choice), and the two bitters. Fill shaker with crushed ice to frappé.

This is a special cocktail featured by Solari's, manufacturers of Greenopal, the absinthe substitute that gives this cocktail its foundation. The name green opal comes from its lovely opalescent color.

A different, highly recommended cocktail for those who want something very good as well as very different.

Jitters Cocktail

> 1/3 jigger ojen
> 1/3 jigger gin
> 1/3 jigger French vermouth

Pour all ingredients into a barglass filled with ice. Jiggle with a barspoon until well frappéd, and serve in a cold cocktail glass.

This is a Spanish cocktail featured by Fernandez & Co., famous Ojen distillers of Jerez, Spain. Barkeepers who claim that Ojen should not be mixed with other liquors, say this one ought to give anybody the "jitters."

Old and odd names for Ojen in New Orleans were *"Majorca"* and *"Anis del mono,"* Majorca for the famous Spanish island in the Mediterranean, and *Anis del mono* meaning "monkey anise." Why monkey? Your guess is as good as mine. Maybe enough Ojen cocktails encourage monkeyshines!

Thirty-nine

Ojen

> 1 jigger ojen
> 1 glass crushed ice
> 1 ounce carbonated water

Fill a barglass with crushed ice. Add a jigger of ojen. Jiggle energetically with a barspoon for a moment or two. Add an ounce of seltzer or other charged water and jiggle again. Strain into a cocktail glass which has been thoroughly chilled.

Ojen possesses so much delicacy of flavor that it should be served neat and not mixed with other ingredients, although there are recipes that call for mixing. While an Ojen is supposed to be frappéd with a spoon, a good shaking will do no harm to the flavor and will induce a thicker coating of frost.

Ojen (which is pronounced *oh-hen*) is a word shortened from the Spanish *ajenjo* (*ah-hen'ho*) meaning absinthe and wormwood in the musical tongue of Spain. It is manufactured from anise, which is also a predominant ingredient in absinthe, and despite its original Spanish name, Ojen contains no harmful wormwood.

Ojen Cocktail

> 1 jigger ojen
> 2-3 dashes Peychaud bitters
> seltzer water

Stir the mixture in a barglass with ice, add a little seltzer or other charged water, and strain into a frappéd cocktail glass.

The bitters give this Ojen a delicate rose-colored tinge. Therefore it masquerades under the name of "Pink Shimmy," or *pinque chemise,* if you prefer the language of the fifty million who can't be wrong.

Suissesse

1 teaspoon sugar
1 pony French vermouth
2 ponies absinthe substitute
1 white of egg
½ pony *crème de menthe*
2 ounces charged water

Mix the sugar with charged water, vermouth, and absinthe. Drop in the white of egg. Fill the glass with cracked ice and shake vigorously. Strain into a champagne glass in which there is a cherry with *crème de menthe* poured over it.

Suissesse, a perfectly good French word meaning a Switzerland-born female, lives up to the reputation earned by those hardy daughters dwelling among the rocks of their picturesque land. The Alps are wonderful—so is a Suissesse. If the name stumps you, pronounce it "swee-cess" and you'll make the barkeep understand what you want. If you yearn to mix one yourself, follow the directions given above and find out why some folk call a Suissesse tops in mixed drinks.

Green Opal Suissesse

The Suissesse given above is probably what originated Swiss yodelling. In New Orleans we have a variation of the happy mixture that transforms yodelling into the more American "whoopee!" Follow these directions for an adventure in excitement:

1 jigger Greenopal or other absinthe
   substitute
½ pony anisette sirup
   white of an egg
   crushed ice

All go into a metal shaker. Shake until the outside takes on a heavy frosting. Bear in mind that one egg white will take care of ten or a dozen portions. Serve in cocktail glasses.

"The Infamous Liquor, the name of which deriv'd from Juniper-Berries in Dutch, is now, by frequent use from a word of midling length shrunk into a Monosyllable, Intoxicating Gin." 1714.

Gin Drinks

Of all popular alcoholics, gin probably leads in favor, especially in tropic and sub-tropic countries. To go high hat with the language, gin is an aromatized potable with a characteristic flavor derived from the juniper berry. The word "gin" is merely a shortening of the liquor's original name, *geneva,* taken from an old Dutch word, *genever,* a name for the juniper berry.

In old writings (such as one of 1706: "Geneva, a kinde of Strong Water, so called") are found many references to this liquor. Its shortened form *Gin,* formerly denoted a double distilled spirit of British manufacture, imitation of the original liquor, marketed by the Dutch as *Hollands geneve,* later known as *Hollands,* but today called Holland Gin.

That the British form of *geneve* was for many years even as now a popular drink, is amply proved by literature of the past. For example, in 1709: "The Gypsie With Flip and Geneve got most Damnably Typsie", and in 1728, Dean Swift, driving home a simile, wrote: "Their chatt'ring makes a louder din than fishwives o'er a cup of jin."

Our so-called dry gin, usually coupled with the information on the bottle that it is "London Dry Gin," as popular in this country and the British possessions, as it is in the Merry Old Isle. First made in England by a redistillation process repeated frequently before bottling, it is quite different from the old Holland gins which verge on the sweet side.

Fable tells us that the name "Old Tom" Gin, of certain British brands, was so named when an old Tom cat fell into a barrel of the spirits. This tradition is antedated by the fact that years before the tale of the drowned cat went the rounds, Hodge's Distillery in England named their brand of gin for old Tom Chamberlain, a distiller employed by them. His picture in the garb of a sailor appears on the labels pasted on the bottles.

Sloe Gin, used in some of our fancy mixed drinks, is named for a small, bitter black wild plum, the oil of which is used to flavor the distilled spirit—not because there is anything slow about its effects. Sloe gin is fast coming into favor because of its mild strength and the distinctive flavor given it by the sloe berries—tart yet somewhat sweet.

Practically all of the gin drinks, the drys, Old Toms, and sloes, belong in the tall glass category . . . tall ones that tinkle when filled with ice and make hot days coolish and hot nights cooler. Before you try any of the famous New Orleans recipes which have for their basic ingredient good old gin, first let me introduce you to a mixed drink that has won world-wide acclaim—New Orleans' own and truly refreshing Ramos Gin Fizz.

Ramos Gin Fizz

1 tablespoon powdered sugar
3-4 drops orange flower water
½ lime—juice only
½ lemon—juice only
1 jigger dry gin
1 white of egg
1 jigger rich milk or cream
1 squirt seltzer water
2 drops extract vanilla (optional)

Mix in a tall barglass in the order given; add crushed ice, not too fine as lumps are needed to whip up the froth of the egg white and cream. Use a long metal shaker and remember this is one drink which needs a long, steady shaking. Keep at it until the mixture gets body—"ropy" as some experienced barkeepers express it. When thoroughly shaken, strain into a tall thin glass for serving.

This gin fizz long has been an institution in the city care forgot. The age of the Ramos gin fizz is well past the half-century mark and its popularity shows no signs of abating. In the good old days before the federal government was so prodigal with padlocks, the saloons of Henry C. Ramos were famous for the gin fizzes shaken up by a busy bevy of shaker boys. Visitors, not to mention home folk, flocked in droves to the Ramos dispensary to down the frothy draft that Ramos alone knew how to make to perfection. One poetical sipper euologized it thus: "It's like drinking a flower!"

Exactly what went into the making of a Ramos gin fizz always has been more or less a secret. One thing is certain—only at the Ramos establishment could one get what tasted like a real gin fizz. Wherefore, like all successful drinks, the Ramos fizz was widely imitated but never really duplicated. Possibly no other thirst assuaging emporium gave the mixture the long deliberate shaking it received from the shaker boys behind the Ramos bar, and that was the secret of its lip-smacking goodness. Came prohibition, and the drink that made the name of Ramos famous disappeared. After the return of legal liquor the trade name of Ramos on a gin fizz was acquired by the Hotel Roosevelt, and today that is its legal domicile.

The gin fizz, and by that I mean the common or garden variety, had its beginning way back yonder, but the Ramos concoction was not known to Orleanians until 1888 when Henry C. Ramos came to New Orleans from Baton Rouge and purchased the *Imperial Cabinet* saloon from Emile Sunier. The *Cabinet* was located at the corner of Gravier and Carondelet streets (where a modern *Sazerac* saloon now holds forth) and above it, on the second story, was a famous restaurant of days gone by—*The Old Hickory*. Here it was that Henry Ramos served the gin fizz that departed so radically from the other frothy gin mixtures served in New Orleans saloons, and here he remained until 1907 when he purchased Tom Anderson's *Stag* saloon opposite the Gravier street entrance to the St. Charles Hotel.

The new place became a mecca for the thirsty and for those pioneers who would make a pilgrimage of any sort for a new drink. At times *The Stag* became so crowded that customers were forced to wait an hour or more (or so it seemed) to be served. The corps of busy shaker boys behind the bar was one of the sights of the town during Carnival, and in the 1915 Mardi Gras, 35 shaker boys nearly shook their arms off, but were still unable to keep up with the demand.

The recipe given is the original formula. Veteran barkeeps differ violently—practically come to blows—over the inclusion of the two innocent drops of *extract of vanilla*. Old-timers who worked for Henry Ramos in the past declare the original Ramos included no vanilla in its make-up. Others hold that the twin drops of extract wrung from the heart of the vanilla bean either make or break a real gin fizz—make it taste like heaven or the reverse.

Therefore, when you mix your fizz, add the two vanilla drops or leave them out, just as you please. If still in doubt, take it up with Paul Alpuente at the Hotel Roosevelt bar. He was with Henry Ramos for years and when he mixes your Ramos gin fizz, watch him closely.

Tom Collins

    1 barspoon powdered sugar
    1 lemon—juice only
    1 dash orange flower water
    ½ lime—juice only
    1 jigger dry gin
    2 ounces seltzer water

Into a tall highball glass place a generous spoonful of bar sugar. Squeeze in the juice of a lemon. Add a dash of orange flower water, and squirt in about 2 ounces of seltzer. Stir until the sugar is dissolved. Next squeeze in the juice of half a lime and add a generous jigger of gin. Stir. Add several lumps of fine ice and jiggle with a barspoon. Add just enough seltzer to fill to the brim and jiggle energetically. Serve in the mixing glass.

Who was Tom Collins? No matter—especially on a hot summer day when you need the coolest, the most refreshing drink known to sweltering humanity. Whether or not you know anything about Mr. Collins or his antecedents, or why he was important enough to have a drink named for him, you can take our word for it that this one is among the best known and best liked drinks in New Orleans, and all points West, East, and North.

Like many another thirst-quencher, the Tom Collins is subject to infinite variations. It is not difficult to concoct and no knack is needed to make it just right, but we implore you not to leave out the dask of orange flower water. Depart not from the recipe above, sanctioned by John Swago, one of the best old-time mixologists who ever pushed a Tom Collins across polished mahogany.

Then there is Rum Collins, or "Charley Collins", which found its way into New Orleans from Cuba. To make this one substitute Cuban type rum, Bacardi or like brands, for the dry gin, but don't leave out the dash of orange flower water.

John Collins

        1 barspoon powdered sugar
        1 lemon—juice only
        1 dash orange flower water
    1/2 lime—juice only
    3-4 jigger rye whiskey
    1/4 jigger rum
        2 ounces seltzer water

A John Collins is made exactly like the Tom Collins with one exception . . . use no gin. The same amount of sugar, lemon, orange flower water, lime and seltzer. Substitute for the gin three-quarters of a jigger of rye whiskey plus one-quarter jigger rum. Mix, stir, and ice in the same way you fixed up Brother Tom, and there you have a cooling summer drink, preferred by many to the one named for Tom Collins.

Gin Fizzes

Silver, Golden, and Royal Fizzes

1 lemon—juice only
1 barspoon powdered sugar
1 jigger dry gin
seltzer water

Mix in a bar glass, drop in several lumps of ice, cover with a shaker and shake well. Pour into a tall serving glass and fill with seltzer water.

The above is the common or garden variety of gin fizz, in which that old standby gin plays the principal rôle, and is not to be confused with the celebrated Ramos gin fizz that has helped contribute to New Orleans' fame.

As with other popular drinks, the gin fizz lends itself to endless variations. We have the Silver Fizz, the Golden Fizz, and the Royal Fizz—a trinity of throat-ticklers in which the addition of an egg, in its separate and collective parts, makes the difference.

A Silver Fizz is made exactly like the gin fizz given above—with the addition of the white of an egg. Shake well in a shaker, remembering that largish pieces of ice are needed whenever any part of an egg is added to a mixture.

A Golden Fizz is identical with the above, save that the yolk only of the egg is used.

A Royal Fizz requires both the yolk and white of the egg.

In any of these gin fizzes it must be remembered that the fizz water is added to the drink after it has been shaken and strained into the serving glass.

Dry Martini

1 pony French vermouth
1 pony dry gin
½ teaspoon orange bitters

Mix in a barglass with several good sized lumps of ice and stir with a barspoon—never put a dry martini in a shaker, as William Powell and Myrna Loy did in *The Thin Man*. Be sure to use French *brut* or dry vermouth if you want your cocktail to crackle. Don't forget the olive! A small pearl onion may take its place if you're onion-minded. Spear the olive (or onion) with a toothpick for dainty transfer from hand to mouth.

Visitors who know their liquor will soon discover that in no other one city does the man behind the bar mix a better dry martini than in New Orleans. That is because the bartender makes a simple operation of it, using the better French makes of dry vermouth, such as Noilly Prat, Cinzano, and Cazapra; and dry gins like Gordon's, Hiram Walker's, Gilbey's, Milshire's, Fleischmann's, Silver Wedding, or similar brands. When making your own, use a good make of orange bitters. Do not shake. We repeat—*do not shake,* even if you heard us the first time. Stir, and serve in a chilled glass.

The dry martini was originally called the "Waldorf-Astoria cocktail" as it was first made of French vermouth (not the sweeter Italian brand) at that famous old New York hostelry in the gay '90's. The recipe called for a dash of orange bitters, 1/3 French vermouth, and 2/3 dry gin . . . olive, of course.

John Swago, of the St. Regis, who knows what he is about when concocting a dry martini, uses dry gin and French vermouth in equal portions, and not the 2/3 gin and 1/3 vermouth usually suggested in drink recipes. Drink one of John's dry martinis and taste the difference!

Forty-nine

Not-Too-Dry Martini

1-2 dashes orange bitters
2/3 French vermouth
1/6 Italian vermouth
1/6 dry gin

This one is for those who prefer their martini cocktail not too dry and not too sweet. *Stir* as directed in the dry recipe with several pieces of ice. Strain into serving glass on top of an olive. Note that this martini is darker in color and a trifle on the sweet side.

This one is frequently termed "the perfect martini."

Sweet Martini

1 part dry gin
2 parts Italian vermouth

This is the one to mix if a sweet martini is what you want. Stir and serve as directed for the dry martini, but do not include an olive when you strain it into the cocktail glass.

The Italian vermouths are not as dry as those made in France and are classified as "sweet" vermouths. A favorite Italian vermouth is that manufactured by Martini & Rossi, which vermouth, by the way, gave this cocktail its name. *Vermout* is a French word applied to a liquor manufactured from white wine flavored with certain aromatic herbs. In this country we spell it *vermouth.*

Wallis Blue Cocktail

1 pony Cointreau

1 jigger dry gin

1 lime—juice only

Mix in a shaker well supplied with pieces of ice. Shake. Strain into a cocktail glass, the rim of which should be rubbed with the lime pulp and dipped in sugar just before being filled and served.

When radio and newspapers blazoned to the world that the Duke of Windsor had concocted a new cocktail at *Château de Cande,* Monts, France, in honor of his marriage to the Lady from Baltimore, many recipes purporting to be THE one found their way into print— most of them impossible.

The former Edward VIII of England toasted his duchess-to-be in what proves to be a variation of the well-known and popular "Side Car" cocktail, with gin substituted for brandy. That the cocktail might match the eyes of his American bride and reflect her penchant for blue, vegetable dye was added to give the proper color. Truly a royal gesture.

The king who surrendered a throne for the woman he loved, mixed a delightful and well-balanced cocktail. You can do the same, if Cointreau is used. While there are a number of satisfactory domestic cordials of the distilled orange type, it is better to stick to the imported brand of M. Cointreau, of Angers, France. Do not substitute lemon juice for lime, and be sure you use a good brand of dry gin. The blue coloring matter isn't absolutely necessary—but it looks pretty and matches Wally's eyes.

Side Car Cocktail

1 jigger cognac brandy
1 pony Cointreau
1 lime—juice only

Pour into a mixing glass with cracked ice and shake well. Strain from the shaker into a cocktail glass, chilled before serving. The imported French Cointreau will be found superior to domestic brands.

This is the Cointreau drink upon which the Duke of Windsor based the "Wallis Blue" cocktail he created at the prenuptial dinner for his bride.

Some prefer lemon when making a Side Car to the tangy flavor of lime. Others make it by using one-third each of brandy, curaçao, and lemon juice. Some substitute Triple Sec for the Cointreau. All are mighty good. One thing to bear in mind when mixing and serving the Side Car is that it must be well frappéd. Therefore, never use cocktail glasses that have not been well chilled in advance.

Legend has it that this cocktail was created by accident. An innkeeper of France, confused and excited by news of damage to his side car, combined separate orders of cognac brandy, Cointreau, and lemon juice into a single drink. The mischance proved a bonanza, for the happy mixture found instant favor. Growing in popularity through the years, Side Car has now become the smart drink of two continents.

Vieux Carré Cocktail

½ teaspoon benedictine
1 dash Peychaud bitters
1 dash Angostura bitters
1/3 jigger rye whiskey
1/3 jigger cognac brandy
1/3 jigger Italian vermouth

The benedictine is used as a base and also for sweetening the cocktail. Dash on the bitters, then add the rye, brandy, and vermouth. Put several lumps of ice in the barglass. Stir. Twist a slice of lemon peel over the mixture. Drop in a slice of pineapple and a cherry if you wish and serve in mixing glass.

This is the cocktail that Walter Bergeron, head bartender of the Hotel Monteleone cocktail lounge, takes special pride in mixing. He originated it, he says, to do honor to the famed *Vieux Carré,* that part of New Orleans where the antique shops and the iron lace balconies give sightseers a glimpse into the romance of another day.

Orange Blossom

1 pony orange juice
2 ponies dry gin
1 dash Peychaud bitters

This drink calls for a shaker. Allow plenty of ice lumps and be sure the mixture is well frappéd before pouring into cocktail glasses previously chilled.

A simple drink to mix and simply grand to drink, especially on a hot day or a warm night. Some devotees of this cocktail prefer a half-and-half mixture of gin and orange juice, and some forego the delight of the dash of Peychaud bitters in favor of the addition of a little grenadine sirup or a little honey. Some make it by using a third each of gin, Italian vermouth, and orange juice.

Whichever recipe you follow, be sure you have a sweet juicy orange. We recommend Louisiana Sweet—the best on the market.

Rickeys

                    1 jigger dry gin
                    or
                    sloe gin,
                    rum,
                    rye whiskey,
                    bourbon whiskey,
                ½ lime—juice *and* pulp
                    seltzer water

Mix in the 6 or 8 ounce highball glass in which it is to be served.
Fill with crushed ice and squirt on the seltzer or other sparkling
water. Remember the lime pulp is left in the glass.

Rickeys must have lime juice in their composition,
whether they are made with dry or sloe gin, Cuban type
rum, rye or Bourbon whiskey. Use plenty of ice cubes
when mixing, don't fail to include the squeezed-out lime
pulp, and liven with selzer water. Any of the waters
which do queer things to your nose will answer.

All we know about the naming of this simple, satisfy-
ing summer drink which comes to us in a tall glass with
clinking ice, is that it was named for a certain Colonel
Joseph Rickey. Another allegation is that he was a
member of Congress!

State Street Cocktail

                1 jigger unsweetened pineapple juice
                1 lemon—juice only
                ½ lime—juice only
                1 jigger dry gin
                1 white of egg
                2 teaspoons sugar

Mix sugar with the gin and pineapple juice until dissolved. Add
juice of the lemon and lime. After placing in shaker with plenty
of ice lumps, add the white of egg—remembering that one egg
will do for a dozen portions. Shake vigorously, as with all drinks
containing egg white. Serve in clear crystal glasses. This drink
is as pleasant to the eye as to the palate with its pale amber color
and collar of foam.

This is the author's favorite warm weather cocktail. He

is fond of it in the wintertime, too. In fact, he doesn't know any season when it fails to hit the spot. His wife brought the original recipe back from Mexico under the name of *"Franco,"* but the author found by experiment that gin was a great improvement over *pulque, mescal,* or *tequila* in mixing the drink.

We always improve 'em in New Orleans. How true what they say about Dixie!

Bronx Cocktail

½ dry gin
¼ French dry vermouth
¼ Italian vermouth
1 thick slice orange
1 dash Peychaud bitters

The Bronx is far from being a dry cocktail, but neither is it too sweet. As the flavor depends upon the orange, it would be well to select a Louisiana Sweet, if possible. The tall barglass should be filled with shaved ice and, with the metal shaker over it, given a vigorous shaking before contents are strained into the serving glass. Some add a dash of Peychaud or Angostura bitters to the mixture before serving.

Just why this particular mixture was christened the Bronx remains a mystery and probably always will. It is quite possible some inspired soul concluded that if Manhattan had its own particular cocktail there was no good reason why the Borough of the Bronx should not similarly be honored.

Like the Manhattan, there are a number of favored recipes for the Bronx, varying in the quantities of gin, vermouths, and orange used. The recipe given above is the one usually served in New Orleans, and when a Louisiana Sweet orange is used, the stranger in our midst learns that a Louisiana-grown Valencia is much juicier and sweeter than the oranges which come to us from Florida or sunny California. (Florida and California papers please copy.)

Old Hickory Cocktail

1 pony French vermouth
1 pony Italian vermouth
1 dash orange bitters
2 dashes Peychaud bitters

Pour the two vermouths into a barglass, add the dash of orange bitters, the two shots of Peychaud bitters. Fill with cubes of ice and stir well. Strain into a serving glass. Twist a piece of lemon peel over then drop it into the glass.

According to hoary but unsubstantiated tradition, this was the favorite tipple of General Andrew Jackson when he was in New Orleans the winter of 1814-15 helping pirate Jean Laffite win the Battle of New Orleans.

But we can promise this Old Hickory cocktail won't be as tough on your palate as was "Old Hickory" Jackson on the British that historic Eighth of January.

Pink Lady

1 pony dry gin
1 pony applejack or apple brandy
1 lime—juice only
2 barspoons grenadine sirup
1 white of egg

Use a barglass for mixing. The amount of grenadine used will determine the sweetness of the drink as well as the pinkness of the lady. The white of egg, which will do for one or a dozen drinks, improves its smoothness. Use large lumps of ice in the shaker. Serve in chilled cocktail glasses.

There are ladies and ladies, but this one, named for a light opera, makes everything rosy.

Another with plenty of championing boy friends is concocted thus: two barspoons of grenadine or raspberry sirup, a jigger of gin, white of egg, and three dashes of Peychaud bitters. Prepare in a shaker glass and exercise your arms, for this one is "To the Ladies!"

Clover Club

1 jigger dry gin
½ lime—juice only
1 pony raspberry sirup
1 white of egg
1 dash Peychaud bitters

Pour the ingredients into the shaker in order given. Drop in the lumps of ice. Set yourself for a good shaking, for this is a cocktail that must be well frappéd. To give chic to the final result, decorate your cocktail glasses with sprigs of mint after straining into them the delightful liquid from your shaker.

Some of the how-to-mix'em-experts use grenadine sirup instead of the raspberry. Upon experiment it will be found that red raspberry not only gives a prettier pink color but imparts a flavor grenadine cannot match. As it has the white of an egg in it, this cocktail must be well shaken.

Why was it named a *clover* cocktail? Well, you have us there. Possibly it's because the lucky recipient, after tossing it off (or should this drink be tossed?) will concede that the finding of a four-leaf clover is not so lucky as finding this cocktail.

We have always admired the added *ummph* the dash of Peychaud bitters gives this deservedly popular concoction.

Alexandre

1 pony dry gin
1 pony crème de cacao
1 pony rich cream
1 white of egg

Have just enough shaved or finely pounded ice in the shaker before pouring in the gin, crème de cacao, and cream. Remember that one white of egg will do, whether you are mixing for two or a dozen guests. Be strenuous in your shaking whenever there is white of egg or cream in a mixture. Shake, brother, shake, and then shake some more for good measure. Strain into cocktail glasses and hear your guests call you a good mixer.

Smooth as cream, delicate as dew, and easily prepared is the Alexandre. Some who mix this particular cocktail do not use the white of egg. A mistake, for the albumen gives a froth and an added smoothness which makes this cocktail different. Like all drinks in which egg white is used vigorous shaking is required. Give the Alexandre all you've got in elbow grease to make it live up to its reputation—for it is truly Alexander the Great among drinks in its class.

Note our Frenchy spelling. If you have trouble with its pronunciation, simply hold your nose tight between thumb and forefinger. But, should you by mischance pronounce it Alexander—it will taste just the same. And the taste is simply de-lovely.

"The chiefe fudling they make in the Islands Barbados is Rum-bullion, alias Kill-Devil, and this is made of sugar canes distilled, a hott, hellish, and terrible Liquor." 1651.

Rum Drinks

From time immemorial rum has been distilled as a by-product of the manufacture of sugar in all countries where sugar cane is grown. As a liquor it became the accepted beverage practically everywhere that strong drink was in demand, and with the spread of its popularity all lusty liquors, regardless of origin, were termed "rum."

In the early days blackstrap molasses, from which rum was distilled, was shipped from Jamaica, Puerto Rico, Santo Domingo, Cuba, and the Barbados into staid New England. True rum is a spirit distilled from "dunder" and molasses. Dunder is taken from the Spanish word *redundar,* meaning overflow, and applied to the lees or dregs of cane juice used in the fermentation of rum. The word "rum" is an abbreviation of *rumbullion,* meaning tumult or uproar—not an inappropriate application! North American Indians had their own name for the drink—they called it *"coow woow"*, a sort of improvement on their customary war whoop.

Remember the ditty sung by the pirate crew in Robert Louis Stevenson's *Treasure Island?*

"Yo ho ho and a bottle of rum!"

Cuba holds the palm for producing the best rum, although staid old New England has made excellent rum from imported blackstrap molasses since 1680, and Louisiana's sugar plantations today contribute their share of excellent domestic brands. More than a century ago Louisiana's rum masqueraded under the name of *tafia.*

"There's naught, no doubt, so much the spirit calms as rum and true religion." Lord Byron's Don Juan, 1819.

Bacardi Cocktail

1 teaspoon sugar
1 lime—juice only
1 jigger rum Bacardi

Mix in a barglass. Muddle the sugar and lime juice thoroughly before adding the rum. Fill with cracked ice. Shake well and then strain into a cocktail glass.

You and I may argue a lot and get nowhere regarding the proper pronunciation of the word Bacardi, but after sampling this cocktail, there'll be no argument as to its effect and authority. It is by far the best way to serve sugar cane rum, whether bottled in New England, Cuba, Jamaica, Puerto Rico, or Louisiana.

In making a Bacardi cocktail be sure to use lime, not lemon, and put no grenadine or other flavored sirup into the mixture. When you shake a Bacardi, frappé it long and well, for it must be served very cold to get the delicious flavor of the *rumbullion*.

Bacardi rum received its name from the Bacardi family of Cuba, well-known distillers and bottlers at Santiago of this particular brand. The correct pronunciation is *ba-car-de'*.

Daiquiri Cocktail

1 teaspoon grenadine sirup
1 lime—juice only
1 jigger rum

Like the Bacardi, the Daiquiri should be well shaken; lime juice, not lemon, should be used to furnish the tang. The grenadine sweetens the cocktail and gives it color. Shake well with ice and strain into the serving glass.

The Daiquiri, like the Bacardi, is a Cuban importation and is very popular in Havana as well as New Orleans.

Again like the Bacardi its name is truly Cuban, Daiquiri being the name of a city in the southeastern part of that famous island not very far from Santiago.

The two cocktails are quite similar, the difference lying in the inclusion or omission of the grenadine sirup. Both are good. Daiquiri is pronounced *Dah-ke-ree'*.

Frozen Daiquiri

    1 lime—juice only
    1 teaspoon sugar
    1 dash white maraschino liqueur
    1 jigger rum

Place the lime juice and sugar in an electric mixing cup, dash on the white maraschino liqueur, and add the rum. Fill half full of finely crushed ice (shaved ice won't do) and place cup under the electric mixer. Let it *whirr* until the mixture is well frappéd . . . until it is practically a sherbet. Strain in a saucer-shaped champagne glass using an ordinary kitchen wire strainer. Shake from side to side and tap rim of the strainer with spoon to force the fine icy particles through the mesh.

During the good old summertime a new sort of cocktail, with rum for its basis, has taken New Orleans by storm—a sort of snow storm. If you have not met the Frozen Daiquiri just picture a champagne glass filled with snow, cold as Christmas, and as hard as the heart of a traffic cop.

You'll have to have something beside the old reliable cocktail shaker to produce this one. It must be whirred to its icy smoothness with an electric drink-mixer—the kind used in making a malted milk.

It is also called "West Indies Cocktail."

Cuban Presidente

½ jigger rum
½ jigger French dry vermouth
1 teaspoon grenadine sirup
1 dash curaçao

Rum first in the barglass, then the vermouth, curaçao, and sirup. Put in the ice. Stir (never shake). After straining into the serving glass, add a piece of orange peel.

This is the drink to toast the Cuban *presidente* (who ever he may be at the present moment). A heady salute for a nation's head. It might be mentioned that some prefer their *presidente* with grenadine only and without the curaçao.

New Orleans Presidente

1 tablespoon grenadine sirup
1 jigger rum
1 tablespoon orange juice

Shake with ice, lots of it cracked fine, and strain into a cocktail glass.

American Presidente

1 pony rum
1 pony French dry vermouth
1 lemon—juice only
1 dash curaçao
1 dash grenadine sirup

Proceed as with the Cuban *presidente* and drop a maraschino cherry into the cocktail glass before straining the mixture into it.

Today several brands of rum, made from Louisiana sugar cane molasses, are finding favor . . . even among those who have long believed that rum, to be good, must come from Cuba, Jamaica, or Puerto Rico.

Grog

2 ponies rum
water
ice

Pour the rum into an 8-ounce tumbler, add ice, and fill to the brim with water. Stir. Drink.

In the old days in Louisiana, especially in that section settled by the British, Irish, and Scottish pioneers, the tipple in high favor was called "grog." It was made of the locally distilled *tafia* or rum, and was dispensed by the British plantation owners of the Feliciana district as a cheap yet potent beverage to slaves who worked the cotton fields. Many references to the drink are to be found in tattered documents written during the days of the Spanish domination. It was set down in them as *"mezcla de arguardiente con agua."*

In 1753 the French of New Orleans knew rum as a *drogue* (a cheap or sorry commodity) and, while it was known as *tafia,* it was also called *guildive* (divine fermentation), and *eau de vie sucré,* meaning "sugar brandy".

The name "Grog" was derived from "grogram," a material of rough texture, ordinarily of camel's wool, used in the making of cloaks. The designation came about in this way: In 1740 Admiral Edward Vernon liberally diluted with water the rum he served the sailors aboard his frigate. It was the admiral's custom to wear a grogram cloak in foul weather, and for this reason the tars called him "Old Grog" behind his back. Forthwith his tars derisively termed the weakened drink "grog," and the name has stuck through the centuries, as witness "grog shop," likewise "groggy," indicating the unsteady gait that follows a too-liberal sampling of spirits.

Planter's Punch

2 lumps of sugar
1 dash Peychaud bitters
1 lime—juice only
1 jigger water
2 jiggers rum

The Planter's Punch calls for a tall glass. Squeeze the lime juice on the sugar. Add the bitters, water, the two full jiggers of rum; fill the glass with shaved or crushed ice. Frappé well with a long-handled barspoon. Sift a little nutmeg on top or a dash of red pepper if you don't mind the bite.

The southern planter had something there! If this man-sized drink were indeed part of a planter's life on a Southern plantation, there was more to his routine than cotton bolls, sugar cane, slaves, and offspring. As we have all along contended, good old sugar cane molasses rum was the planter's stand-by, notwithstanding traditional tales of the huge consumption of Monongahela red whiskey.

Jamaican Planters' Punch

1 part lime juice
2 parts sugar
3 parts Jamaica rum
4 parts water and ice

A doggerel for this recipe runs: "One of sour, two of sweet, three of strong, and four of weak," thus making it easy to keep the proportions in mind. This is Planters' Punch as it is made in Kingston, Jamaica, British West Indies, where the rum is manufactured. For the regulation Planters' Punch a dash of Peychaud bitters must be added. Shake and serve very cold.

Mississippi Planter's Punch

1 tablespoon sugar
1 lemon—juice only
½ jigger rum
½ jigger Bourbon whiskey
1 jigger cognac brandy

Dissolve the sugar with a little water in a mixing glass. Add the lemon juice, then the rum, Bourbon, and brandy. Fill with fine ice, clap on the shaker, and go to work. When well frappéd pour into a long thin glass. Decorate with fruit (if you want to be swanky) and serve with a straw.

If this cooler doesn't make a Mississippi cotton planter forget about the boll weevil, charbon, and high water, give up trying to make him forget. All that is lacking in the recipe is a shady gallery, a rocking chair, and a palmetto fan.

Tangipahoa Planter's Punch

1/3 pineapple juice
1/3 orange juice
1/3 lime or lemon juice
1 teaspoon grenadine sirup
2 jiggers rum

After mixing and sweetening to taste with the grenadine, add the fruit juice, the two jiggers of rum, and put plenty of ice in the tall glass. Jiggle with the barspoon until well frappéd.

"Aw, nertz!" said a friend of mine who likes to furnish his inner man with certain powerful potables several times a day, "the dope you wrote on the opposite page ain't a Planter's Punch! Leastwise," he hedged, "it ain't what we folks up in Tangipahoa call a Planter's Punch."

As a result of this criticism I cajoled from him the above recipe. Ever notice how all recipes for Planter's punches call for two jiggers, and never one, of rum? That, you'll agree, is a redeeming feature. So don't be thrifty with the oh-be-joyful when you concoct a punch by this or any other recipe.

Viva Villa

1 lime—juice and pulp
1 scant spoonful sugar
1 generous jigger tequila

Dissolve sugar in a little water. Squeeze on the juice of a green lime and drop in the pulp of half the lime. Next the jigger of tequila and fill to the brim with finely cracked ice. Jiggle with the spoon until well frappéd. A pinch of salt brings on the flavor.

Tequila is a native Mexican liquor distilled from the Century plant, which also supplies the Mexicanos with *mescal,* another powerful potable. The drink gets its name from the Tequila district where the Century plants (*Agave tequilana*) are cultivated for the fermented juices they yield. Tequila is practically colorless—but don't let that fool you.

All you need to make this drink perfect is a sombrero and a señorita. Omit the sombrero if necessary, but don't leave out the señorita!

Rum Runner

1 jigger rum
1 spoon sugar
2 ponies pineapple juice (unsweetened)
1 lime—juice only
1 dash Peychaud bitters

Dissolve the sugar in the unsweetened pineapple juice. Squeeze in the juice of a lime (lemon will answer but it doesn't give quite the flavor a lime does). Then the bitters and muddle well. The jigger of rum is added. You may stir this drink with several lumps of ice but shaking improves it and the white of an egg gives it added smoothness.

During the unlucky thirteen years that Prohibition darkened the land, the rum runner was the only little ray of sunshine on an otherwise sombre horizon. What more appropriate than a demon rum drink be named for this angel of mercy?

The hostess who strives to give her guests something deliciously different can do no better than fix upon a Rum Runner. But she must be prepared for many repeats. They always come back for more.

If you want a Pilgrim's Progress—substitute grapefruit juice for the pineapple juice. Then you'll know why the Pilgrim fathers came over on the Mayflower, landed on Plymouth Rock, and entered into the business of distilling rum from molasses. It was to provide our ancestors with the Spirit of '76.

Jean Laffite Cocktail

1 teaspoon sugar
2 dashes absinthe substitute
2 dashes curaçao
1 jigger rum
1 egg yolk

Mix in a barglass. The absinthe goes on the sugar, then the curaçao. Muddle. Add the jigger of rum and drop in the egg yolk. Clap on shaker and go to it. Strain into a chilled cocktail glass.

Let us hope that when Jean Laffite, the bold, bad, Barataria buccaneer, swaggered up and down the narrow *banquettes* of *rue Royale* he had something like the above in mind. Hardly, however, as it was years post-dating the Laffite regime before *absynthe* cast its greenish glow over Crescent City bars, and how it desolates us to think of Jean, brother Pierre, Dominique You, René Beluche and the balance of the doughty crew of smugglers going thirsty for the lack of an Absinthe House.

Whether or not Jean Laffite ever sampled the cocktail

now bearing his name is open to violent debate. We think he did not, but we often meditate on the possible change in Louisiana history had he done so. Drink enough Jean Laffites and you'll be all set to jump into a pirogue and paddle up the bayou all by yourself.

Legend tells us that the favorite tipple of the Laffites and others of their ilk was a noggin or two, or three, of a distinctive and potent beverage called *le petit goyave,* brewed from the fermented juice of the fruit of the aguava or century plant and toting the kick of an army mule. In Mexico the same liquor is called *pulque.* It was served at the *Café des Réfugiés* in Saint Philippe street, a tavern where was ever assembled a motley crew of swiggers—*colons de Saint-Domingue,* West Indian seamen, *révolutionnaires,* filibusters, and Kentucky flatboatmen.

Host Jean Baptiste Thiot mixed another curious drink which he called "The Pig and Whistle." Years later, in 1835, when Thiot deserted the St. Philip street location and opened a new eating and drinking tavern in Old Levee (Decatur) street opposite the French Market, he called the new tavern after his famed mixed drink—"The Pig & Whistle."

Pousse Café

There are two schools of thought regarding the naming and spelling of a Pousse Café, but only one regarding its goodness. Properly made it becomes a drink with more rings than an old-fashioned Barnum & Bailey circus. Here we have a post-prandial drink made of layers of variously colored cordials—the heaviest poured first into the serving glass and the following layers gently and skillfully achieved one ring at a time with the aid of a spoon. The lightest liqueur, usually cognac, is poured on last.

The name *Pousse café* is said to have been derived from *chasse café,* literally "chase coffee" or a "coffee chaser," a potion of liquor taken after a meal ostensibly to remove the taste of coffee, tobacco, or what have you. The term, usually shortened to *chasse,* was applied as a rule to brandy, *crème de menthe,* or like cordials, but in time became definitely attached to the ringed drink of various cordials, now known as *Pousse café.*

For another (and probably more authentic) version: *pouce,* French for "inch" or "thumb," indicates that in the early days of the original concocting of the drink, an inch or *pouce* of red sirup was first poured in the glass; then a *pouce* of curaçao, then a *pouce* of chartreuse, and so on to the final *pouce* of brandy that topped it. Thus it became a *pouce café* or "inch" drink, until finally the word *pouce* was corrupted into *pousse,* a French word with an entirely different meaning.

"So one glass of cognac neat, as a chasse (to more things than claret)." 1857.

Pousse Café

1/6 red raspberry sirup
1/6 pink maraschino sirup
1/6 green crème de menthe
1/6 orange curaçao
1/6 yellow chartreuse
1/6 topaz cognac brandy

Care and skill are essential in the making. Use a short, transparent round glass and put in each cordial separately, also very, very slowly so as to eliminate blending. The heaviest of the sirups is poured in first to form the bottom ring. Ease in with a spoon, so that the liquid will not fall with force enough to mix with the preceding ring. The last or top ring is of cognac. When completed the drink will be composed of six different rings, each complete in itself. Lovely!

Santini's Old New Orleans Pousse Café

1/4 cognac brandy
1/4 maraschino sirup
1/4 curaçao
1/4 Cuban rum

Proceed as above, but watch your step. The main difficulty will come in gently layering a heavy sirup on top of the lower ring of brandy, which in usual recipes, is the top or finishing ring.

This is the drink that was vogue in New Orleans in 1852 when Joseph Santini opened his "The Jewel of the South" saloon in Gravier street opposite the side entrance of the old and fashionable Saint Charles Hotel. It is said to be the first *pousse café* with both brandy and rum.

Triple Pousse Café

1/3 curaçao
1/3 chartreuse
1/3 cognac brandy

Easily made, so it is suggested that the amateur mixer

try his hand on this one before experimenting with the multiple-ringed kinds. It has all the delights of the more intricate *pousse cafés.*

Cuban Rainbow Pousse Café

1/8 grenadine sirup
1/8 anisette
1/8 abricotine, apricot brandy, or apry
1/8 crème de menthe
1/8 orange curaçao
1/8 yellow chartreuse
1/8 green chartreuse
1/8 Cuban rum

The preparation of this *pousse café* is the same as given in the recipes. Note, however, that this rainbow of liqueurs calls for a ring of rum to top it (brandy may be substituted). Set afire with a match and the rainbow will be a blaze of color.

This is the *Pousse café* that Sloppy Joe of Havana, Cuba, serves customers at his famous bar, a rendezvous for convivial New Orleanians and other travelers.

Tchoupitoulas Street Guzzle

1 split ginger beer
1 jigger Cuban type rum

Ginger beer is not to be had these days, but ginger ale will do as well. Mix with ice.

Guzzle is a somewhat inelegant word meaning to drink immoderately or frequently. Prior to the Civil War days the *Iron Horse* tavern was famed for its guzzle. As it increased in popularity along a certain New Orleans street it acquired the name of that street and became known as the Tchoupitoulas Street Guzzle. Tchoupitoulas (pronounced *Chop-a-too'las*) was the name of an ancient Indian tribe that had its village in what is now the upper part of New Orleans. Just what sort of fire-water was their favorite guzzle history saith not.

Seventy-one

"Buy any brand-wine, buy any brand-wine?" London
street cry, 1622.

Brandy Drinks

The name brandy comes from Old Dutch *Brandwijn,*
meaning "burnt (i.e. distilled) wine," and to the end of
the 17th century the old original form, "brandy-wine"
was used. Properly, brandy is an ardent spirit distilled
from wine, although similar liquors distilled from fermented juice of peaches, cherries, apples, or other fruits,
are also called brandies . . . such as peach brandy.

Genuine cognac is recognized as the finest of brandies
and was called cognac from the fact that a superior
brandy is produced at or near the town of Cognac in the
Charente region of France, center of a famous grape
growing territory. For the same reason brandy is better
known today as *cognac* in its native land than by its original French name of *eau-de-vie.* In the United States it
is usually called "cognac brandy."

While the term cognac is loosely applied to any French
brandy, it should be borne in mind that all brandy is
not cognac. Among the better known cognacs are those
of Martell, established in 1715, and that produced by the
firm of James Hennessy, whose bottles carry the familiar
"three-star" designation. In 1765 the original James Hennessy, an Irish adventurer, offered his sword in service
to the French king, and during his fighting days was
stationed in the Charente valley where he became en-
amored of the excellent brandy there produced. When
swords were sheathed, Hennessy settled in this vineyard
country and became a grape-grower, a brandy-distiller,
and a cognac-bottler.

"I was entertained, with Kisses fine, and Brandy Wine." 1719.

Café Royale

In New Orleans a certain coffee drink is often erroneously called a *pousse café*. It is in reality a *Café Royale* or *Café Real,* nothing more or less than black coffee in a *demi tasse* with cognac brandy floated on top.

It should not be called a *chasse café* because basically it is coffee itself, and you can't chase coffee with coffee. The *Café Royale* should not be confused with that other famous New Orleans' after-dinner drink, *Café Brûlot,* the recipe for which will be found on the next page.

Orange Brûlot

1 orange
1 pony cognac brandy
1 lump sugar

Take an orange and lightly slit the peel horizontally through the middle, then turn the rind back and upward to form a cup. Repeat with the other half of rind, reversing the process to form a base. Be careful not to disengage the peel from either end of the orange, and leave the stripped orange pulp intact for the center standard of your natural goblet.

In the upper part of the orange rind or cup place a lump of sugar, then pour in the pony of brandy. Set off with a match and stir while the sugar is dissolving in the blue flame.

Preparing this natural container takes practice and deftness, and the idea of burning the brandy in the orange rind is for the sake of the flavor and oil contained in the peel, besides making a picture that charms with its novelty. The fruit of the orange is delightful to eat after the brandy has been burned and the drink quaffed.

Café Brûlot

1 cup cognac brandy
45 pieces loaf sugar
50 whole cloves
3 pieces stick cinnamon broken in bits
½ orange peel cut thin
1 small piece lemon peel cut thin
1 quart strong New Orleans dripped coffee

Combine the ingredients in advance. In a *brûlot* bowl pour a cup (1/2 pint) of cognac brandy. Add the sugar, cloves, sticks of cinnamon broken in bits, thinly cut orange peel, and sliced lemon rind. The mixture should be set to steep for at least six hours in advance of serving time to allow the brandy, spices, and citrus oils to blend. The coffee is prepared separately and is not mixed with the spiced brandy until serving time. Will serve 20 guests.

A special *brûlot* equipment is required if you are to burn *café brûlot* successfully. This equipment consists of a specially manufactured bowl of silver on copper, a circular tray, and a long-handled ladle, all of the same metal known as Sheffield. Don't use your wife's silver fruit dish, even though it may resemble a *brûlot* bowl in shape and appearance. We know a man who did this in the absence of the little woman, and rich old Aunt Hattie's wedding gift *phiffted* into the shape of Aunt Hattie in fewer minutes than it takes to tell. We hesitate to speak of the fiery aftermath when the storm-and-strife returned.

Put the brandy mixture in the bowl, then pour a small portion of alcohol into the circular tray, just enough to sparingly cover the base of the bowl. The dripped coffee, prepared in advance, is brought to the table steaming hot. All lights in the room are extinguished to accent the *brûlot* flames; the alcohol in the tray is touched off with a match and allowed to burn until the contents of the bowl are heated. Dip up a little of the mixture with the ladle and hold in the flame rising from the tray, then dip ladle in the mixture to hurry the process of ignition.

Stir, lifting the ladle high in the air. A ribbon of golden-blue flame follows the motion, and is a sight to goggle the eyes of the uninitiate. Allow to burn only a few moments as too much burning uses up the alcoholic content. Pour in the coffee, slowly and lovingly.

Serve in after-dinner coffee cups. This recipe makes enough to thrill 20 coffee connoisseurs.

Do not attempt to make *brûlot* with ordinary coffee. Boiled or percolator coffee will not answer. What is known as French or New Orleans dripped coffee must be used and made very strong. Most New Orleans folk prefer chicory in their coffee; which gives a richer color and heavier flavor. Therefore, for *brûlot* use a coffee-and-chicory brand, such as Luzianne, Union, Chase and Sanborn Louisiana Roast, French Market, Morning Joy, etc.

Put coffee in upper receptacle of a drip coffee pot. Just enough boiling water is poured on to moisten and swell the grains. Add boiling water, a spoonful or two at a time, and repeat at intervals until the quantity desired has "dripped" to the lower container of the coffee pot. To keep contents hot until needed, the pot may be set in a pan of simmering water.

Café brûlot (pronounced *ca-fay' broo'lo*) takes its name from two French words—*café*, or "coffee," and *brûlot*, which has dual meanings . . . "highly seasoned" and "incendiary or burning." Both fit the *brûlot* perfectly. In other words, it is "burnt spiced coffee."

Dorothy Dix, who often stirs a *brûlot* at the home of this writer, calls the delectable brew "liquid fruit cake."

Antoine Special

> 1½ jiggers Dubonnet wine
> 1½ jiggers French vermouth

The Dubonnet is poured into a wine or flip glass, and the vermouth skillfully "floated" on—not mixed. This appetizer is best without the addition of bitters or even ice. The flavor of the Dubonnet is improved by chilling—but avoid diluting with ice cubes.

This is the *apéritif* featured by Antoine's, oldest and most celebrated French restaurant in New Orleans. It was Jules Alciatore, son of Antoine Alciatore founder of the famous rendezvous of gourmets, who originated this inspiring before-dinner appetizer. Simple to make—easy to take . . . there you are; one whiff of this rhythmic fluid makes poets of us all.

Jules, like his illustrious sire, has passed on to his well-deserved reward. But when you dine at this St. Louis street shrine to Epicurus you will flatter the house by specifying *Antoine Special* as your appetizer.

Stirrup Cup

> 1 lump sugar
> ½ lemon—juice only
> 1 jigger cherry brandy
> 1 jigger cognac brandy
> 1 maraschino cherry

When you have dissolved the sugar in a little water add the lemon juice, and the two brandies. Stir with ice and strain into a cocktail glass. Drop in the cherry.

It occurs to us that in a day when the motorcars have outstripped horseflesh, "runningboard" cocktail would be a more suitable name for this delectable parting cup.

The above recipe compounds a farewell drink potent enough to make you fancy yourself on a horse, feet in stirrups, yelling "giddy-yap," and ready to go places and do things. Origin has been attributed to George Washington. If true it may be the reason the father of our country departed on such frequent trips from *Mount Vernon*. Another clue—there's a cherry in it!

Father, mother, sister, brother we cannot tell a lie—this is a swell drink. No wonder G.W. was first in the hearts of his countrymen.

Ambrosia

> 1 jigger cognac brandy
> 1 jigger applejack
> 1 dash cointreau
> 1 lemon—juice only
> champagne

Mix all but the champagne and pour into a thin 6-ounce glass. The mixture will half fill the glass. Pour in the champagne to the brim. Drink while sparkling.

Ambrosia is popularly supposed to have been the drink concocted by the Greek gods on Mount Olympus, and was calculated to put sparkle in Grecian ladies' eyes and hair on Grecian gentlemen's chests. At *Arnaud's,* one of the better French restaurants in New Orleans' *Vieux Carré,* a modern version of the Mount Olympus is served. We have it from the proprietor, Arnaud Cazenave ("Count Arnaud" to his familiars) that the ambrosia he brews is one the lovely Hebe might well have served Juno, Jupiter, Ganymede, and the balance of the Olympus crowd. We who have sampled it agree.

(Note by our dietetics editor: Ambrosia was the *food* partaken of by the high gods of Olympus. Nectar was the *drink.*) No matter—ambrosia or nectar—it's all one at the incomparable Arnaud's.

"A Goodly Countrey . . . abounding with wild Date trees . . .
whence they draw a liquor called Tarrie." 1609.

Toddies, Slings, and Flips

While we apply the name *Toddy* to that drink in which we mix whiskey, gin, rum, or brandy with a little sugared water, the original toddy was a far different drink from that which we now imbibe under the same name.

"Toddy" originally was the fermented sap obtained from the incised spathes of various species of palms, especially the wild date palm, and used as a beverage in tropical countries. A Hindustani word, *tari* in the beginning, it later became *tarrie*, then *tary, terry, tadie, taddy, toddey, toddie* and, finally as we know it today, *toddy*.

Toddy is just another name for Sling, or vice versa. For example a Hot Whiskey Sling calls for a lump of sugar in a half-glassful of boiling water, a jigger of whiskey, a small piece of lemon peel and a grating of nutmeg. Now if you want a Hot Whiskey Toddy, duplicate the above and omit the nutmeg.

Some like'em hot, some like'em cold, some like'em with gin, some with brandy, some with Scotch. But in any case the addition or omission of nutmeg makes the difference between toddy and sling.

The Kentucky Toddy is composed of a lump of sugar, a little water, a twist of lemon peel, a full jigger of Bourbon, a lump of ice, and a lot of stirring.

"Toddy, originally the juice of the cocoa tree and afterwards
rum, water, sugar, and nutmeg." 1788.

Flips

The Flip was at one time a hot drink served in an earthenware mug, much favored in England and America before tea and coffee came into common use. The drink was composed of ale, egg, nutmeg, sugar, ginger, and brandy or rum. It was made sizzling hot by heating an iron loggerhead, or flip-dog, in the fire until it was red-hot and thrusting the heated end into the mug of mixed liquor, whence a sound like *"Sz-z-z-t!"* resulted, and a vapor like heaven arose.

The flips of today have gone cold, and the flip-dog remains chilled and neglected by the fireplace, its solitary use now to poke the burning logs. Ice has taken the place of heat in the various concoctions carrying the ancient name. Some of these, relics of a past, are given below.

Ale Flip: Beat up an egg with a half-teaspoon of sugar, fill the glass with ale, mix well with a spoon and grate nutmeg on top.

Brandy Flip: Fill the glass half-full with crushed ice. Put in one egg, one jigger brandy, a teaspoon of sugar. Beat until it froths and grate nutmeg on top.

In similar manner is made a Rum Flip, a Gin Flip, a Sherry Flip, or a Whiskey Flip. A Yankee Flip has a jigger of apple brandy added to the egg and sugar. All must be topped with grated nutmeg.

"The first craving of an American in the morning is for ardent Spirits mixed with sugar, mint, or some other hot herb, which are called slings." 1807.

Slings

A Sling, so we are told by long-ago writers, is "an American drink composed of brandy, rum, or other spirit, and water, sweetened and flavored," and had nothing to do with "the slings and arrows of outrageous fortune", so feelingly bespoken by Hamlet in his morose soliloquy.

As long ago as 1788 a certain shipwrecked scribe recorded that he and his mates found "a case-bottle filled with Holland's [gin], of which each of us took a sling." This indicates the word originally had the same meaning as "draught," "pull," or "swig," as Americans describe the swigging of a healthy mouthful from a jug.

A Bitter Sling, quite a favorite in the old days as an electioneering potion, was described in 1806 thus: "a stimulating liquor composed of spirits of any kind, sugar, water, and bitters."

Singapore Sling

½ jigger dry gin
½ jigger apricot brandy
½ jigger cherry brandy
½ lime—juice only
seltzer water

To sling this drink you must first provide yourself with a highball glass nearly filled with cracked ice. In it squeeze the juice of a lime, then add the gin, cherry brandy, benedictine, and all that can go in of seltzer water. Frappé with a spoon, or in a shaker. Garnish with fruit.

This is a drink that makes you itch to travel—or anyway step out. In olden times a drink was slung from one mug to another in mixing, and that's how the Sling derived its name. The word itself came from the Low German *slingen,* which means to swallow.

Here's slinging at you.

Sloe Gin Singapore Sling

1 jigger sloe gin
1/2 jigger dry gin
1/2 jigger apricot brandy
1/2 jigger cherry brandy
1/2 lime—juice only
1 teaspoon sugar

Mix in a 12-ounce highball glass. First the sugar, then the lime juice, the two brandies, the two gins. Stir, fill two-thirds with cracked ice, and fill to the brim with seltzer. Decorate with a slice of orange, a slice of pineapple, and a cherry.

Stone Fence

1 jigger rye whiskey
sweet cider
3 lumps ice

Pour the jigger of whiskey in a tall glass, drop in the three lumps or cubes of ice and fill to the brim with the unfermented cider. All left to do is to stir and sip.

Washington Irving, in his Diedrich Knickerbocker's *History of New York,* claimed the Dutch-Americans were inventors of "sherry-cobbler" and "stone-fence," and in 1809 Irving also claimed that the original settlers of New Amsterdam were responsible for the naming of the "cocktail."

Why whiskey and sweet cider, joined in holy wetlock should figure under so unemotional a name as "stone-fence" is matter for deliberation. One punster quips: "Drink enough and you'll overcome all obstacles and never take offense."

Originally the name "stone-fence" was applied to an applejack and sweet cider combination, and those in the know will tell you that as sweet cider ferments it develops into applejack.

However it may develop one thing is certain—it's one of the hard liquors that is powerfully easy to take.

*"A glass of swizzle, the most salubrious beverage in
hot weather."* 1843.

Swizzle

The name Swizzle has been applied to variously compounded drinks, and while it is said the origin of the
word is unknown it appears to be just another way of
pronouncing Switchel, a drink made of molasses and
water, sometime with the addition of vinegar, gin, and
rum. Also applied to strong drinks sweetened and
flavored with bitters.

To make a Swizzle a swizzle-stick is necessary—a
round wooden stick or dowel with swollen bottom end
from which protrude five smaller sticks like the spokes
of a wheel. The swizzle-stick is rotated rapidly between
the palms to mix the drink thoroughly. A Swizzle,
according to legend, is a liquid institution of Demerara,
British Guiana, and became quite popular in the West Indies before it made its appearance in Old New Orleans.
There were many references to the drink over a century
ago, such as "The boys finished the evening with some
fine grub, swizzle, and singing." (1813), and a British
traveler, Lady Brassy, more intrigued with the way the
drink was concocted with a swizzle-stick than with the
drink itself, wrote in 1885: "I mean to take home some
'swizzle-sticks.' They are cut from some kind of creeper,
close to a joint, where four or five shoots branch out at
right angles, so as to produce a star-like circle. The whole
is mixed with powdered ice, and stirred or 'swizzled' until
it froths well."

As early as 1800 this same drink was known as Switchel, an Englishman noting that "the dauntless Yankees
still drank their switchell," so that derivation of *swizzel*
from *switchel* seems plain.

*"We were never 'groggy', 'intoxicated', 'swizzled', or 'tight',
but once."* 1843.

Swizzle

1 wineglass rum
1 tablespoon "New Orleans" molasses
1 pony water
2-3 dashes Peychaud bitters

Mix in a barglass, swizzle with a swizzle-stick, add ice, swizzle again. Strain into a serving glass.

This is the summer swizzle; in the wintertime piping hot water is added to the rum and molasses. Rotate with the swizzle-stick, and grate a little nutmeg on top. Serve the hot drink in the mixing glass.

Sangaree

½ teaspoon sugar
1 jigger port wine
nutmeg

Mix the sugar with the port wine before filling the mixing glass nearly full of fine ice. Stir vigorously, or put the mixture in a shaker. Strain into a thin glass and grate a little nutmeg on top.

While the original recipe for Sangaree calls for port wine, it is sometimes made with brandy, sherry, gin, or even ale. The drink is a tropical one and because of its color derives its name from the French *sang*, meaning "blood." We are also told the name "sangaree" fits any drink, so long as it's red, and made of wine and sweetened water, then spiced and iced. The drink is an old-fashioned one and was very popular as a guest refreshment in old Creole days.

"At Nerule is made the best Arach or Nepa de Goa, with which the English on this Coast make that enervating Liquor called Paunch (which is Indostan for Five) from Five Ingredients." 1672.

Punches

Punch is the ideal beverage to serve at large gatherings and many are the kinds from which to choose when you are preparing to entertain in a big way.

The Punch Bowl, or Bowl O'Punch, as our English cousins call it, has long been a feature of Christmas and holiday festivities. The word punch comes from India, and is derived from the Hindu *panch,* meaning five, the original beverage being composed of five ingredients, viz.: spirits, water or milk, lemon, sugar, spice or cordial. The punch field is covered by arrack, brandy, claret, gin, milk, rum, tea, whiskey, wine, and fruit punch. The drink is usually qualified by the name of the principal ingredient, as, for example, whiskey punch.

St. Charles Punch

1 teaspoon sugar
1 lemon—juice only
1 jigger port wine
1 pony cognac brandy
1/3 teaspoon curaçao

Dissolve the sugar with a little water in a mixing glass. Add the lemon juice, the port wine, the cognac, and last the curaçao. Fill the glass with fine ice and jiggle with the barspoon. Pour into a long thin glass, garnish with fruit, and serve with a straw.

Years ago this was a famed punch very much in demand at the celebrated St. Charles Hotel bar. Don't omit the straw; this drink demands long and deliberate sipping for consummate enjoyment.

Orgeat Punch

½ jigger orgeat sirup
1 lemon—juice only
½ lime—juice only
1 jigger rye whiskey
1 dash orange bitters
1 pony port wine

Mix all but the port in the order named in a tall 12-ounce glass. Fill with cracked ice to a finger-width of the top. Jiggle with a spoon until well frappéd. Then float on top the pony of port wine . . . do not stir.

Says Sam Guarino, chief bartender at the Hotel Roosevelt bar, who originated this drink delight, "The Orgeat Punch has two distinct flavors which register separately when trickling down your throat. First you taste the Oporto, then you get the second rich taste of the orgeat-flavored whiskey mixture."

Orgeat sirup, or *sirop d'orgeat,* is made from the milk of almonds and has long been a favorite flavoring and sweetening liqueur among the Creoles of New Orleans. It is not used as much today as in the past, but drink-mixers who like something different should cultivate its acquaintance again.

Arrack Punch

1 jigger date arrack
2 teaspoons bar sugar
2 dashes lemon juice

Dissolve the sugar in a little water, add the lemon juice, then the arrack; fill the glass nearly full with shaved ice, and shake well. Strain into a glass and serve with a straw.

Arrack is the fermented juice of the date palm, and is a name that was applied in Eastern countries to any spirituous liquor of native manufacture, especially ones distilled from the fermented sap of the coco-palm, or from rice and sugar fermented with cocoanut juice. Later the arrack imported from Batavia and Japan was considered superior in concocting the punch, at which time the name arrack was shortened to "Rack."

Arrack punch was a favorite tipple in the New Orleans of the splendid idle 40's when flourished W. J. Logan's "Pelican" coffee-house "at Gravier and Union in the rear of Clapp's Church," as he always advertised his place. The Pelican's specialties were Arrack Punch and Pineapple Julep, both mixed in huge bowls and prepared fresh every day. As a punch it bears no resemblance to the mixtures we now call by that name, and the Pineapple Julep of Host Logan came nearer being a punch than the drink designated today as julep.

Pineapple Julep

> 1 quart sparkling Moselle wine
> 2 jiggers dry gin
> 2 jiggers maraschino sirup
> 2 jiggers raspberry sirup
> 2 oranges—juice only
> sugar to taste
> slices pineapple

This punch, for it is not really a julep according to our modern acceptation of the term julep, should be prepared by placing a large piece of ice in a punch bowl and pouring on the mixture then ladling it over the ice long enough to melt some of the ice and chill the whole. The pineapple should be the fresh fruit, if possible, and sliced over the bowl. Cherries from the maraschino bottle, strawberries, and other fruits in season can be added. This recipe makes enough for six servings.

In the days of old, the days of gold, and the days of '49, when embryonic miners flocked through New Orleans on their way to the newly-discovered California gold fields, these same would-be miners found many places in the Crescent City to wet their whistles. One popular oasis was Logan's "Pelican Coffee-house," told of in the foregoing page, where the Arrack Punch and Pineapple Julep were counted the best in town.

Louisiana Party Punch

1 quart rum
1 pint lemon juice
1 pint strong tea
2 pints carbonated water
½ pound granulated sugar

This recipe makes one gallon of punch—sufficient for 12 guests, depending upon capacity. Make the tea quite strong and allow it to cool. Mix the ingredients and pour into a gallon jug the day before serving as this will promote blending and enhance the flavor and bouquet of the punch. Have it well chilled by placing the jug in the ice box.

When party time arrives put a large piece of ice in the punch bowl with slices of orange and lemon and other fruits in season. Serve to your guests in regulation 5-ounce punch cups.

"When the steward cometh in at the hall doore with the wassell, he must crie three tymes, Wassell, Wassell, Wassell." 1494.

The Wassail Bowl

The Wassail Bowl contained liquor in which healths were drunk in the long ago, the favorite content being the spiced ale used in Christmas eve and Twelfth-night celebrations. The custom of brewing a Wassail bowl has fallen into disuse and is revived only rarely.

The word "Wassail" used of old when presenting a cup of wine, or drinking a comrade's health, carried the same meaning as "hail" and "farewell." The reply to the salutation "Wassail," when presenting the bowl of wine, was "Drink-hail," in accepting it.

Sang Sir Walter Scott in his *Lay of the Last Minstrel* "The blithesome signs of wassel gay, Decay'd not with the dying day."

Wassail Bowl

2 baked apples
2 tablespoons fine sugar
1 tablespoon allspice
1 lemon, juice and peel
1 quart hot ale
1 pint warm sherry

To make the Wassail Bowl bake two apples and cut in small pieces. Add the sugar, the allspice, the lemon, the heated ale, and warm sherry. Mix well, mashing with a muddler, heat and serve hot.

The Wassail Bowl is as significant of Christmas as is St. Nicholas himself. After sampling, who shall say there ain't no Santa Claus? Perhaps, indeed, it was the original Wassail Bowl that inspired this loveliest myth of childhood, when out of good fellowship engendered by the mellowing Christmas brew, the spirit of Christmas took shape in the hearts of men.

Hail the Wassail Bowl! We know there's a Santa Claus!

Eighty-eight

Eggnogs

As long ago as in the period when Shakespeare wrote his plays we find chronicled: "Nog is a kind of strong beer brewed in East Anglia." In writings two hundred years later we find records of such a brew as "egg-nog" in which "the white and yolk of eggs are stirred with hot beer, cider, wine, or spirits."

In 1825 New Yorkers read in a newspaper called *Brother Jonathan,* that "the egg-nog had gone about rather freely" at a certain party. A score of years later A. O. Hall, stopping at the old St. Charles Hotel while in the Crescent City gathering material for his *Manhattaner in New Orleans,* popular book of its day, "trembled to think of the juleps, and punches, and nogs, and soups," consumed in the dining-room of that famed hostelry.

Much liquor has flowed over the bars since Nog was originally described as an ale brewed in East Anglia, now modern Norfolk and Suffolk in England. Every egg-nog recipe today calls for milk or cream; none for ale or hot beer. Time changes everything. Blessed be time for some of the changes it makes in our cups of cheer!

Following are recipes for the best eggnogs we have ever tasted.

"The sailor toasts thy charms in flip and grog; The Norwich Weaver drinks thee deep in Nog." 1774.

Eighty-nine

Sidoux's Holiday Eggnog

6 eggs
6 tablespoons powdered sugar
1 cup granulated sugar
½ pint brandy
½ pint rum
2 pints heavy whipping cream

First beat the egg yolks well, add the cup of granulated sugar slowly, and then just enough of the cream to give the mixture a pale lemon color. Next add the brandy and rum, beating hard while the liquors are poured in. Whip the remaining cream and add. Then whip the egg whites dry and add the powdered sugar and fold—do not beat—into the mixture.

The Creoles have "little" names for the people and things they love, and Sidoux (pronounced *See-doo,* and meaning "so sweet,"), is a love name bestowed upon a little girl we knew. She isn't a little girl any longer. She has grown up and developed into the World's Number One cheer dispenser and above is her prescription for speeding up holiday merriment. It is as sweet as her name and a lot less innocent.

Sidoux tells us this Christmas mixture will keep in the ice box for many days. (Note by author: only under lock and key.)

Whiskey Eggnog

1 jigger whiskey
1 raw egg
1 cup thin cream
1 spoon sugar

Mix in barglass, pour in shaker half-filled with fine ice and shake well. Strain in a thin glass and grate nutmeg on top. Brandy or rum can take the place of whiskey.

There you have the eggnog in its simplest composition—but good to the last drop. Try it for proof.

As we have warned you, there are many recipes for genuine *nogs* brewed in the modern manner—a far cry from the ale and cider styles in vogue in Merrie England a century or two ago.

Tom And Jerry

eggs
sugar
brandy
rum

Take as many eggs as the number of drinks you expect to serve and beat the whites to a stiff froth. Add one heaping teaspoon sugar for each egg white. The egg yolks are beaten separately. Mix the whites and yolks and sugar together with a pinch of bicarbonate of soda and place in a large bowl, stirring occasionally to prevent the sugar from settling.

To serve: Take two tablespoons of the above mixture and put in a crockery mug. Add 1/2 jigger brandy and 1/2 jigger rum, fill to the top with hot milk or cream (or boiling hot water). Stir with a spoon and grate a little nutmeg on top.

Runner up for holiday honors is this celebrated drink named for the two titular characters in Pierce Egan's book, *Life in London, or days and Nights of Jerry Hawthorne and his Elegant friend Corinthian Tom,* a fictional pair of rakes and sporting bloods of the Regency period in Merrie England. First appearing in print in 1821, the book's two characters took on new fame with the naming of this instantaneously popular drink in their honor, and with the fact that drinking places became "Tom and Jerries" instead of tap rooms.

When and how the drink found popularity in America or when it was first served in New Orleans is not known, but references to it appeared almost a century ago.

White Ribbon Punch

(FOR 12)

2 cups sugar
2 cups water
2 cups orange juice
2 cups grape juice
1 cup lemon juice
8 cups iced water
4 cups iced tea

Boil sugar and water 4 minutes. Cool. Add rest of ingredients. Serve in glasses half filled with cracked ice. Top with mint leaves.

What! no liquor? Skip it if you feel that way about it, but we had to think of the fellows who have been ordered off of alcohol, and the ladies who are giving a party for the preacher.

Afterthought: Candied cherries, lemon and orange slices can be frozen in the ice cubes used for this punch if one has a mechanical refrigerator. The effect is decidedly artistic, and the goodness is decidedly enhanced.

Jack Rose Cocktail

1 lemon—juice only
1½ teaspoon grenadine sirup
1 jigger applejack brandy
2 dashes Peychaud bitters

Mix in barglass or directly in shaker. Add ice lumps and shake. Serve in cocktail glass. In spite of similarity of names this favorite was not named for the New York gangster. Jack Rose is merely our way of saying Jacqueminot rose—which the finished drink resembles in color.

Ninety-two

Canal Street Daisy

¼ lemon—juice only
½ lime—juice only
2 dashes grenadine sirup
1 jigger rye whiskey
1 squirt carbonated water

Mix in a silver mug, pewter tankard, or highball glass. Fill with finely crushed ice and jiggle with spoon until well frosted. Decorate as you like with fruits or mint sprigs. Serve with a straw. This is a pre-prohibition favorite that is coming back into favor. A Gin Daisy is made the same way—merely substitute gin for the rye whiskey.

Stinger

2/3 jigger cognac brandy
1/3 jigger white crème de menthe

Mix in barglass, shake well with lumps of ice, and strain into chilled cocktail glass.

Widow's Kiss

½ pony yellow chartreuse
½ pony benedictine
1 pony apple brandy
2 dashes Peychaud bitters

Half fill a mixing glass with shaved ice. Add the chartreuse, benedictine, apple brandy, and bitters, then shake well. Serve in a cocktail glass.

Between-the-Sheets

½ jigger rum
½ jigger cognac brandy
½ pony triple sec or Cointreau
1 lemon—juice only

This mixture is to be well shaken with cracked ice and served in a cocktail glass, cooled in advance.

Ninety-three

The Contradiction

1 barspoon sugar
½ lemon—juice only
1 jigger rye whiskey

Mix in a barglass. Fill with cracked ice. Clap on the shaker and shake vigorously before straining into a cocktail glass.

This is the drink a Frenchman had in mind when he walked into a New Orleans cocktail lounge and said to the man behind the bar:

"Mix for me, *s'il vous plait,* a contradictions."
"A which?" demanded the puzzled barkeep.
"Zee great Américain drink—a contradictions."
"Never heard of it, mister . . . how's it made?"

"You use whiskee to make eet strong; water to make eet weak; lemon juice to make eet sour, an' sugar to make eet sweet," explained the French visitor. "Zen you say: 'Here to *you.*' an' you drink eet yourself! Zat, sar, ees zee contradictions."

Whereupon the barkeep mixed the drink—which you will have no difficulty in recognizing as the old reliable, time-tested Whiskey Sour.

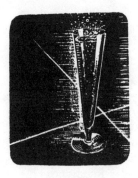

I N D E X

To Be a Good Mixer, Remember:

jigger equals _____ 1½ ounces

pony equals _____ 1 ounce

tablespoon equals _____ ½ ounce

barspoon equals _____ 1 teaspoon

barglass equals _____ 3½ ounces

dash equals _____ 20 drops or
1/3 teaspoon